What's With Atlanta?

Paige Watts

Enjoy discovering Atlanta!

Cheers,

Paige Watts

REEDY PRESS

DEDICATION

For Kevin: Atlanta wouldn't be the same without you.

Library of Congress Control Number: 2023938774

ISBN: 9781681064963

All images are courtesy of the author or believed to be in the public domain unless otherwise noted.

Design by Jill Halpin

Printed in the United States of America
23 24 25 26 27 5 4 3 2 1

CONTENTS

PREFACE

ATL. The A. Hollywood of the South. A City in the Forest. Dare I even mention Hotlanta? Whatever you call it, Atlanta is a unique and exciting city!

I've enjoyed writing about all the little things that make Atlanta special. This book is by no means a full history or a complete guide. It's more of a taste: an introduction to this incredible city and the people, culture, and quirks that make the ATL what it is.

The history isn't always pretty (it never is in the South), and the idiosyncrasies aren't always easy to explain. But when we take it all in, we get a clearer picture of the diverse and vibrant city Atlanta is today. The city has come a long way from its roots as a small railroad town. Atlanta is an amalgamation of its past transgressions and continuing growth, its traditional Southern foods and international cuisines, its bustling city streets and lush natural spaces.

There's a lot to learn about Atlanta, and I hope this book inspires you to go out and explore new neighborhoods, dig into the truth behind some of your favorite locations, and continue to make the city a better place to live in and to visit.

Whether you've lived here your whole life, are a new transplant, or are just visiting, you can learn something new about what makes Atlanta Atlanta. Read on to learn the ins and outs of navigating the city, where and what to eat, the need-to-know history and the little-known secrets, and all about life in Atlanta.

Paige Watts

Atlanta Begins at Its End

Terminus and other names for Atlanta

Atlanta has always been, and continues to be, a transportation town. The city was founded in 1837 as the end of the Western and Atlantic train line from the Midwest to Georgia. The zero milepost for this terminus was marked between what are now Forsyth Street and Andrew Young International Boulevard. By 1842, homes and a general store were built up around the area, the planned terminus was moved four blocks southeast, and the settlement became known as Terminus.

Once the depot was built in 1842, the settlement changed its name to Marthasville after Governor Wilson Lumpkin's daughter. The town was incorporated on December 23, 1843. In 1845, the chief engineer of the Georgia Railroad suggested yet another name change, this time to Atlantic-Pacifica in honor of the rail line, shortened to "Atlanta", though not a single train had visited yet. Both the governor and the residents approved the name change; fortuitously, Governor Lumpkin's daughter's middle name was Atalanta, so the city is still named for her.

 TRANSPORTATION

The name change to Atlanta was officially approved on December 26, 1845, three months after the first Georgia Railroad trains arrived in the town. The railroad was a major contributor to Atlanta's growth and development. A second railroad, the Macon & Western, completed tracks to Atlanta in 1846, connecting the city to Savannah. In 1851, the Western and Atlantic Railroad finally completed its tracks connecting Atlanta to Chattanooga. In 1854, the Atlanta and LaGrange Railroad arrived to connect Atlanta to the southwest.

Fact BOX

Before it was Terminus, the small settlement around the zero milepost was known as Thrasherville. In 1839, John Thrasher built up homes and a general store at what is now 104 Marietta Street in front of the State Bar of Georgia Building. He also built the Monroe Embankment, an earthen embankment that created a gentle grade between different rail lines, which is considered the oldest existing man-made structure in Atlanta.

What's With All the Peachtrees?

Driving around Atlanta, you'll notice an abundance of streets named "Peachtree," the most famous of which is Peachtree Street that runs through Midtown and Buckhead before it changes names to Peachtree Road, Peachtree Boulevard, and Peachtree Industrial Boulevard.

With 71 street names that incorporate the word "Peachtree," it's a wonder we don't all get lost!

At first glance, you may assume the term comes from Georgia being the Peach State–that is, until you realize there's not a single peach tree in sight.

 TRANSPORTATION

So where did all the "Peachtrees" come from? Historians believe the name comes from what the Muscogee people called the area, Pakanahuili, which translates to "Standing Pitch Tree." Pitch trees, or pine trees with their sticky resin or pitch, are plentiful in Georgia, unlike the peach tree. Throughout the years, either through mistranslation or our Southern drawl, "pitch tree" became "peach tree," and the name stuck.

Fact BOX

Atlanta's other street names were put into place by early settlers, and many of them are centered around water. Creeks and springs are a common occurrence in road names. Streets with "ferry" and "bridge" names (Powers Ferry, Holcomb Bridge) come from the original crossing points to get across the Chattahoochee River. Even Ponce de Leon Avenue comes from Atlanta's own "Fountain of Youth" spring that was believed to have rejuvenating powers.

The Malfunction of Spaghetti Junction

Millions of drivers have to traverse the Tom Moreland Interchange north of Atlanta connecting major roads I-285, I-85, US-23, and Buford Highway. The four-level, crisscrossing interchange is named for the state highway commissioner in the 1970s and '80s, Tom Moreland, who took major steps in restructuring Georgia's interstate system. But Atlantans call it Spaghetti Junction.

The interchange earned its nickname from its mess of overlapping roads that resemble a plate of spaghetti. Despite Moreland's restructuring, Spaghetti Junction remains one of Atlanta's worst spots for traffic. It was named "worst truck bottleneck" by American Transportation Research Institute three years in a row. In 2023, the junction earned the No. 4 spot with an average speed of 28.5 miles per hour during rush hour.

 TRANSPORTATION

Spaghetti Junction isn't the only Atlanta interchange wreaking havoc on commuters' travel times. The Atlanta metro area holds nine of the top 100 spots on the same list. The I-285 and I-20 interchange on Atlanta's westside earned the No. 5 spot, 1-75 at McDonough and the I-285 and SR-400 interchange earned spots No. 13 and 14 respectively, while the I-20 and I-285 interchange on the eastside and the I-285 and I-75 interchange on the northside earned spots No. 17 and No. 18 respectively. Though they're further down the list, the I-20 interchange at I-75/I-85, the I-75 and I-675 interchange, and the I-75 and I-85 interchange still cause plenty of slowdowns for Atlanta travelers. Each of these slowdowns dominos to the rest of the interstates, doubling or tripling the normal commute time in comparison to rush hour.

Fact BOX

Atlanta hip-hop duo OutKast wrote an entire song devoted to Spaghetti Junction on their 2000 album *Stankonia*.

To and Fro on Atlanta Public Transit

MARTA, the Metropolitan Atlanta Rapid Transit Authority, has been providing Atlantans with transit for over 40 years. The dream of a 5-county bus and rail system began in the 1950s and '60s and started to become a reality in 1972 when MARTA took ownership of the Atlanta Transit System, Atlanta's main bus system at the time. Throughout the '70s, work began on creating a rapid rail system, with operation on the East Line beginning in 1979.

Today, MARTA provides service to 1.7 million residents in Metro Atlanta, with people taking about 488,000 trips a day. It has made over 5 billion trips since the start of its service in 1979, making it the eighth largest transit system in the United States based on ridership.

The MARTA bus system is comprised of more than 550 buses that provide service on 101 routes along 1,439 miles of road. The MARTA train system has over 338 rail cars that service 38 stations and rail lines that span over 48.1 miles.

TRANSPORTATION

Trying to get to and from the airport? MARTA has a direct rail line to the Hartsfield-Jackson International Airport, providing easy access from Downtown, Midtown, Buckhead, and everywhere the rail line reaches.

Fact BOX

MARTA's busiest stations based on entries and exits are: Five Points, College Park, Airport, Peachtree Center, and Lindbergh Center.

The Perimeter, Inside and Out

I-285 is a 64-mile loop around the perimeter of Atlanta, hence its nickname: The Perimeter. The interstate was officially opened in 1969 to help travelers on I-75 and I-85 bypass the worst of Downtown Atlanta traffic. But today, it has some of Atlanta's nastiest traffic, with four of its intersections topping lists of the worst traffic bottlenecks. The interstate is a cause of headaches for millions of drivers daily, yet it's an indispensable roadway for those commuting from Metro Atlanta's suburbs.

INTERSTATE
GEORGIA
285

The Perimeter isn't just an interstate—it's also a handy way of describing location. Do you live Inside The Perimeter (ITP) or

 TRANSPORTATION

Outside The Perimeter (OTP)? You can describe where a restaurant or attraction is located by stating if it's ITP or OTP, or just inside The Perimeter or just outside The Perimeter. This can be particularly helpful when a neighborhood traverses The Perimeter, like Sandy Springs or Chamblee. Businesses describing themselves as located south of The Perimeter or north of The Perimeter are common as well.

To some, what lays Inside The Perimeter is the "true Atlanta" and anything OTP doesn't really count. But those of us who know better know that there are some amazing hidden gems Outside The Perimeter that you don't want to miss when visiting Atlanta.

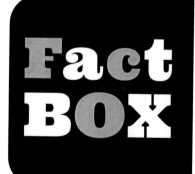

Fact BOX

In 1982, Braves pitcher Pascual Pérez earned the nickname "Perimeter Pascual" when he missed the start of a game because he circled I-285 three times looking for Atlanta-Fulton County Stadium.

Express **In** and **Out** of Atlanta

When the I-85 Express Lanes and Peach Pass opened in 2011 between Chamblee-Tucker Road and Old Peachtree Road, they caused a bit of a stir since they converted existing lanes into paid toll lanes. But in that first month, the state of Georgia issued 100,000 Peach Passes and saw 159,000 trips taken via the toll lanes.

The Peach Pass uses a small transponder that attaches to your windshield. When you pass under the express lane sensor, it automatically deducts the proper toll. The Peach Pass express lanes give commuters a way to bypass the gridlock on Atlanta's most congested interstates and is a worthwhile investment for Atlanta residents who always seem to find themselves stuck in rush hour traffic.

 TRANSPORTATION

Currently, there are Peach Pass lanes on sections of I-85 north, I-75, and I-575. Portions of I-75 and I-575 feature reversible lanes that travel in the direction with the greatest demand and can be adjusted for special events like holiday travel. Additional express lanes along I-285 are currently being added.

Peach Pass lanes are designed to alleviate some of Atlanta's most congested corridors. Their prices change depending on traffic conditions—the price rises as demand for use of the express lanes increases. The reversible lanes allow the express lane to be open only during rush hour times; since peak hours are different on the weekend, the reversible lanes have a different schedule on Saturday and Sunday than they do on weekdays.

Fact BOX

Your Peach Pass can access toll roads in Florida and North Carolina as well.

Hartsfield-Jackson
International Airport

The world's busiest airport

What does it take to be the busiest airport in the world? An average of 2,700 take-offs and arrivals a day, an average of 275,000 passengers a day, and a total of around 110.5 million passengers a year (at pre-pandemic levels in 2019). Hartsfield-Jackson International Airport has been the

world's busiest airport since 1998.

Atlanta's airport is named after two former mayors who had a hand in growing the international hub—William B. Hartsfield and Maynard Jackson. It was built on the site of the old Atlanta Speedway racetrack in 1925 and soon attracted companies like Delta Air Lines and Eastern Air Lines. The Atlanta airport has always been busy.

Courtesy of redlegsfan21 on Flickr

 TRANSPORTATION

And a busy airport needs a big complex. The terminal complex covers 156.1 acres, with a Domestic and an International terminal, seven concourses, and 192 gates. To get from one concourse to another, you could walk through a series of underground connectors with moving sidewalks. Each section is decked out with different art and history installations to make this trek more enticing, like the "Flight Paths" installation between concourses A and B with its multi-colored ceiling and rain shower simulation. For those in a hurry, you could take the Plane Train, an enclosed subway system that connects all the concourses on a three-mile loop track and takes much less time.

But why is Atlanta's airport the busiest? Being the main base and headquarters for Delta Air Lines plays a big role. It also has a strategic location on the east coast, making it a major entry point for international traffic coming into the US. It's a convenient location domestically, too—Atlanta is within a two-hour flight of 80% of the US population.

Courtesy of J. Glover on Wikimedia Commons

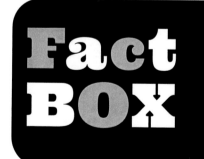

Fact BOX

Hartsfield-Jackson International Airport has the tallest air traffic control tower in North America at 398 feet tall—it's also the fourth tallest in the world.

Atlanta's Choice Airline

Delta Air Lines began south of Atlanta in Macon in 1925 as the world's first aerial crop-dusting operation known as Huff Daland Dusters, Inc. The Huff-Daland Duster was the first true crop-dusting aircraft and was designed to combat the boll weevil infestation that had terrorized cotton crops in the South for nearly a decade. Shortly after it was founded, the company moved to Monroe, Louisiana, and it was incorporated as Delta Air Services, named after the Mississippi Delta region, in 1928.

Passenger operations began in 1929. The company secured an air mail contract over a route that stretched from Fort Worth, Texas to Charleston, South Carolina, and the company grew from there. Atlanta became the headquarters for Delta in 1941. From pioneering the development of the hub-and-spoke system to being the first airline to fly the Douglas DC-8, Convair 880 jets, and McDonnell Douglas DC-9, Delta has consistently stayed ahead of the aviation

 TRANSPORTATION

game. It was even the first airline in the world to board one million passengers in a single city in a month (Atlanta, August 1979).

Atlanta is Delta's primary hub and is its largest hub. Overall, Delta Air Lines has more than 4,000 flights every day, connecting more than 275 destinations on six continents. In Atlanta, Delta sees around 1,400 take-offs and arrivals every day. Some of Delta's most popular routes from Atlanta fly to Orlando, Boston, Los Angeles, and Detroit.

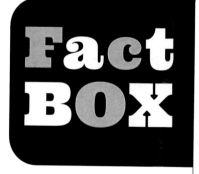

Fact BOX

Delta Air Lines is one of the oldest airlines in the world. It's the oldest US airline still in operation and the 8th oldest airline worldwide.

A Streetcar Named
Downtown
LOOP

The first streetcars in Atlanta operated from 1871 to 1949, beginning with horse- and mule-drawn carriages that caused a mess on the unpaved roads, and then upgrading to open-air electric streetcars running on tracks in the 1880s. Back in those days, Atlanta was a hub of public transportation with a sprawling streetcar system and

Courtesy of Cqholt on Wikimedia Commons

interurban railways to outlying towns. The streetcar system played a huge role in shaping Atlanta's neighborhoods. But in 1949, with the rise in popularity of the personal automobile bringing down passenger numbers, Atlanta ran its last streetcar, opting instead for trackless trolleys and buses that had more freedom of route and stops since they weren't shackled to tracks.

TRANSPORTATION

Fast forward to 2003, and Atlanta Streetcar, Inc. began dreaming of an Atlanta streetcar system once again. In 2012, Phase I of the Atlanta Streetcar Project began with the construction of the Downtown Loop. The 2.7-mile loop officially opened for service on December 30, 2014. The Downtown Loop serves 12 stops in the tourist district from the Martin Luther King Jr. Historic Park to Centennial Olympic Park.

MARTA took control of the streetcar in 2018 and is incorporating it into its plan for a larger MARTA light rail system. There is access to the MARTA train line at Peachtree Center, but plans to expand the streetcar from Midtown to the Northeast, from Downtown to the Southwest, and from Bankhead MARTA to Midtown, and a longer route along Peachtree Street between Midtown and Five Points, have yet to pan out. MARTA hopes to get an expansion eastward from Downtown to the Atlanta BeltLine and Ponce City Market started in 2024 and completed by 2027.

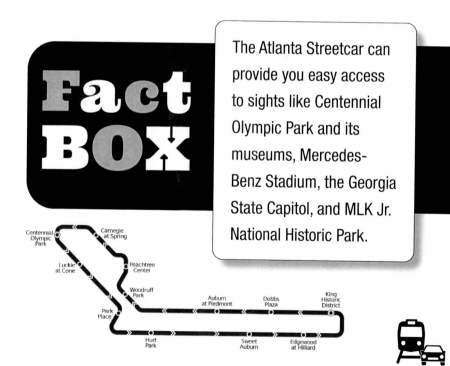

Fact BOX

The Atlanta Streetcar can provide you easy access to sights like Centennial Olympic Park and its museums, Mercedes-Benz Stadium, the Georgia State Capitol, and MLK Jr. National Historic Park.

Atlanta BeltLine

A pedestrian perimeter

The Atlanta BeltLine is the plan to redevelop a former railway corridor around the central part of the city that, when completed, will measure a 22-mile main loop of multi-use trails. BeltLine plans also include a streetcar loop, overseen by MARTA. It is designed to connect many of Atlanta's neighborhoods and communities, improve transportation, add green space to the city, and showcase arts and culture.

The idea for the BeltLine came in 1999 from Georgia Tech student Ryan Gravel, who envisioned a means of alternative transportation in Atlanta. After gaining the support of Atlanta business leaders, work began on the project in 2006. The continuous loop of paved footpath around the city will allow all kinds of non-motorized traffic, including bicycles, roller-skates, and pedestrians. In total, the multi-use paths will measure 33 miles of main loop and spur trails connecting to neighborhoods.

 TRANSPORTATION

As a redevelopment program, the Atlanta BeltLine aims to create a more equitable, inclusive, and sustainable city life. It connects to 45 diverse neighborhoods and communities and has a goal of providing 5,600 units of affordable housing. Plans include creating or improving 1,300 acres of parks and green space around the corridor. The BeltLine has also gained notoriety for its rotating art installations, dance exhibitions, and musical performances, with Art on the BeltLine featuring hundreds of murals and sculptures along the Eastside and Westside Trails.

Underground Atlanta

Back in Atlanta's early days, the five-block area around the original Terminus train depot had become so congested with trains, buggies, pedestrians, and automobiles that the city decided to build viaducts over the streets for automobile traffic. In 1928, the street level was raised by one and a half stories, completely covering the original area. Businesses moved their storefronts up and used the ground floors for storage and, during Prohibition, speakeasies.

As Atlanta continued to grow, the lower level lay forgotten until the 1960s, when the original storefronts and decorative brickwork were rediscovered intact. Work began to redevelop the area as a retail and entertainment district, and Underground Atlanta was born.

As one might expect, the literal underground of a city attracted some seedy activity. Underground Atlanta had about five good years before trouble began to set in. New bars elsewhere in Atlanta generated competition, fights began to break out, crime became uncontrollable, and a new MARTA line took out a third of the new district. Underground Atlanta closed in 1980.

Multiple revitalization efforts by new developers have had little lasting success. In 1989, Underground Atlanta re-opened as a

 ONE-OF-A-KIND TREASURES

Courtesy of Haydn Blackey on Flickr

shopping mall. World of Coca-Cola museum opened here in 1990, and Underground Atlanta was a central celebration point during the 1996 Olympics. Even a 2004 ordinance allowing the district's bars to stay open later than the rest of the city wasn't able to hold people's attention.

Today, the main draw is the Masquerade concert venue in Kenny's Alley. The upper level of Underground Atlanta has plans to host office towers, apartments, and shops. The lower level is attracting the attention of local artists and temporary immersive exhibits that have been able to draw a crowd in for a good time, but not a long time.

Fact BOX

Underground Atlanta renovations left the original facades mostly intact, including a historic gas lamp that was erected in 1856.

GEORGIA Aquarium

When it opened in 2005, the Georgia Aquarium was the largest aquarium in the world. It lost that title in 2012, but it still remains the largest in the US. Bernard Marcus, co-founder of The Home Depot, donated $250 million toward the creation of the aquarium with a vision of Atlanta having an aquarium that encouraged both education and economic growth.

The Georgia Aquarium was designed around a 6.3-million-gallon whale shark exhibit called Ocean Voyager, the largest indoor aquatic habitat in the world. The aquarium was the first and only outside of Asia to house whale sharks due to the difficulties in transporting the species and the amount of space their habitat needs. The Ocean Voyager habitat was designed to hold six full-sized whale sharks; at its opening, the habitat housed only four. They were flown in pairs 8,000 miles from Taiwan on a specially configured UPS 747 freighter outfitted with life-support systems supported by Georgia Aquarium animal care staff to ensure a smooth transition.

 ONE-OF-A-KIND TREASURES

Whale sharks aren't the Georgia Aquarium's only claim to fame. It is also the only aquarium in North America to house manta rays. And the Tropical Diver gallery's Pacific barrier reef habitat is one of the largest living reef exhibits in the US.

The aquarium's more than 10 million gallons of water house thousands of animals. Among those are the rare whale shark and manta rays, but also beluga whales, African penguins, California sea lions, multiple other species of shark, and dolphins. Visitors can view marine life from all sides in an acrylic tunnel, through multiple acrylic viewing windows, and even up close and personal through diving experiences.

Fact BOX

The Georgia Aquarium has a few mascots, one of which is a dolphin named Betty after beloved actress Betty White.

ZOO
Atlanta

From traveling circus to world-class zoo

Zoo Atlanta got its start in 1889 when a failing traveling circus donated its collection of animals to the city of Atlanta. City leaders set up the menagerie in Grant Park, and it's been there ever since. The zoo started out with a small collection of a jaguar, a hyena, a black bear, a raccoon, an elk, a gazelle, a Mexican hog, lionesses, pumas, camels, and snakes. In 1890, the zoo got its first elephant. And the donation of Coca-Cola heir Asa G. Candler Jr.'s private collection in 1935 more than doubled the zoo's residents. Today, Zoo Atlanta has more than 1,000 animals across 220 species.

The zoo hasn't always been the high-class attraction it is today, though. In 1984, after the deaths of several exotic animals, the then-named Grant Park Zoo lost its accreditation and went through a major reformation. In 1985, the zoo officially became Zoo Atlanta and was on the up-and-up.

In 1961, one of Zoo Atlanta's most beloved animals joined the family: a gorilla named Willie B., after Atlanta mayor William B. Hartsfield. He was brought in to replace another gorilla of the same

ONE-OF-A-KIND TREASURES

name at the urging of the mayor. At the time, he was the zoo's only gorilla, and he lived a sad and lonely life in a completely indoor cage with just a TV and a tire swing. Willie B. didn't step outside until 1988 with the installation of the new Ford African Rain Forest habitat. Today, Zoo Atlanta has the largest gorilla and orangutan population in the US. Willie B. passed away in 2000, but he left behind 25 children and grandchildren.

Primates aren't the only animals the zoo is known for. In 1999, the pandas came to town. Zoo Atlanta is the fourth zoo in the US to house these benevolent bears. Two panda bears, Lun Lun and Yang Yang, on loan from China made their debut. By 2016, they had sired seven bouncing baby bears. While most of the bears have been sent back to China, parents Lun Lun and Yang Yang and twins Ya Lun and Xi Lun still remain at Zoo Atlanta.

Cyclorama

The truth about the Battle of Atlanta

Cycloramas were all the rage in the late 19th century–they allowed viewers to immerse themselves into a large panorama painting that surrounded them on all sides, often with music and a narrator telling the story of the painting. There were hundreds of these paintings produced and toured around the globe to purpose-built circular buildings in cities and at World's Fairs. The Battle of Atlanta Cyclorama is one of 17 cycloramas remaining in the world. For over a century, it was displayed in Grant Park at Zoo Atlanta before moving to the Atlanta History Center in 2019.

Atlanta's Cyclorama is 49 feet tall, covers an area of 16,000 square feet, and weighs 10,000 pounds. The painting was created in 1886 in Milwaukee by German artists depicting the Union victory at the 1864 Battle of Atlanta. However, the painting didn't remain that way for long. In 1892, it was relocated to Atlanta and was touched up and modified to appeal to Southern audiences as "the only Confederate victory ever painted". While the Battle of Atlanta was decidedly not a Confederate victory, that perception of the Cyclorama remained for decades.

 ONE-OF-A-KIND TREASURES

With its move to the Atlanta History Center, the Cyclorama has been restored to its original 1886 painting, complete with a multi-media experience full of light and sound describing not only the painting's events but its history and modifications as well. Now, the Cyclorama isn't just a painting but a look at how we interpret the past.

Fact BOX

A familiar face hides in the foreground diorama—the likeness of Clark Gable was added after he and other *Gone with the Wind* cast visited in the 1930s.

Georgia State Capitol

The gold-domed capitol building

Atlanta hasn't always been Georgia's capital city. It's actually the state's fifth capital, the others being Savannah, Augusta, Louisville, and Milledgeville. Even though Atlanta was a major transportation center in the Southeast, it had been rejected as a potential new capital before the Civil War. But the promise of five acres of land and money for a new capitol building proved enticing enough to permanently move Georgia's capital to Atlanta in 1877.

Construction of the capitol building specified that only Georgia materials be used, unless the cost was too expensive. The exterior of the building used bricks salvaged from the old City Hall, Georgia marble for the interior, native pine, iron ore mined in Georgia, and Indiana limestone. The building was constructed from 1885 to 1889 and was completed under budget.

The Capitol has remained largely unaltered except for the addition of its iconic gold dome. In 1959, the citizens of Lumpkin County, the site of Georgia's gold rush, donated gold to gild the dome and lantern of the Capitol. Forty-three ounces of gold made its way via wagon train from Dahlonega to Atlanta. The gold was pressed into gold

 ONE-OF-A-KIND TREASURES

leaf as thin as a gum wrapper. Their mistake in gilding the dome was attempting to adhere the gold in the winter. By 1977, half the gold had deteriorated. Dahlonega held a statewide fundraising campaign, led another wagon train, and delivered another 60 ounces of gold to Atlanta. The dome was regilded in 1981, and any future damage to the gold is repaired as it occurs.

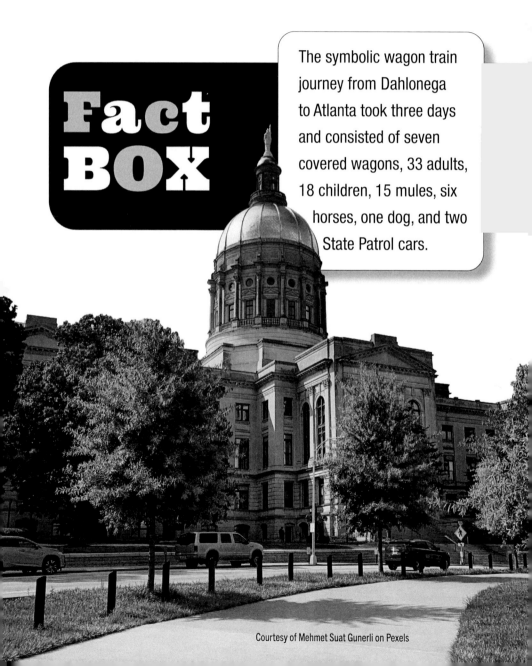

Fact BOX

The symbolic wagon train journey from Dahlonega to Atlanta took three days and consisted of seven covered wagons, 33 adults, 18 children, 15 mules, six horses, one dog, and two State Patrol cars.

Martin Luther King Jr.
National Historical Park

Where a great leader was born

Courtesy of the Library of Congress

An expansive property, Martin Luther King Jr. National Historical Park covers 35 acres and dozens of historical buildings in the Sweet Auburn community near downtown Atlanta. The collection of buildings includes Dr. King's birth home, Ebenezer Baptist Church, and Fire Station No. 6. It was listed as a National Historic Site in 1980, but the site was expanded and designated a National Historical Park in 2018.

 ONE-OF-A-KIND TREASURES

Visitors to the park can find the home where Dr. King was born, the burial place of Dr. King and his wife, a museum dedicated to the American Civil Rights Movement, an exhibit on desegregation in the Atlanta Fire Department, the "I Have A Dream" World Peace Rose Garden, the International Civil Rights Walk of Fame, and a memorial tribute to Gandhi.

Most of the historic buildings in the park were built between 1890 and 1920, and almost all of them have a connection with Dr. King's life and work. Unlike at other National Parks, there is no fee to visit Martin Luther King Jr. National Historical Park. Dr. King's legacy is freely accessible for all to learn about the Civil Rights Movement.

Fact BOX

Sweet Auburn is a historically African American neighborhood where black-owned businesses thrived in the 1940s and '50s. In 1956, *FORTUNE* magazine called Sweet Auburn "the richest Negro street in the world."

National Center for **Civil** and **Human** Rights

The National Center for Civil and Human Rights is an eye-opening museum that explores the American Civil Rights Movement as well as today's global human rights issues. The concept for the center came from Evelyn Lowery, Juanita Abernathy, former Atlanta mayor Andrew Young, and former House Representative John Lewis. The building was designed by architect Philip Freelon on a site at Pemberton Place donated by the Coca-Cola Company. The museum opened on Memorial Day 2014.

There are currently three permanent exhibits at the Center. "Rolls Down Like Water: The American Civil Rights Movement" explores examples of segregation, Jim Crow laws, and significant events in the American Civil Rights Movement. "Spark of Conviction: The Global Human Rights Movement" takes a look at current and past dictators and their human rights violations, modern-day activists who

 ONE-OF-A-KIND TREASURES

are currently working to improve conditions of marginalized individuals around the world, and issues that affect human rights in countries around the globe. Finally, "Voices to the Voiceless: The Morehouse College

Courtesy of Rowland Scherman

Martin Luther King Jr. Collection" presents personal letters and papers that belonged to Dr. Martin Luther King Jr., including instructions for non-violent protests and a collection of King's sermons.

The National Center for Civil and Human Rights is not only a museum but also a human rights organization that hosts performances and lectures. It offers educational programming, human rights training for law enforcement officials, and Diversity, Equity, and Inclusion experiences for workplaces.

Fact BOX

The lunch counter sit-in simulator gives you a moving experience of the types of threats and harassment activists encountered during this form of peaceful protest.

JIMMY CARTER Presidential LIBRARY and MUSEUM

Inside the Oval Office of the only president from the state of Georgia

President Jimmy Carter had an interest in building a Presidential Library in Georgia since taking office in 1977. Construction began on the library three years after Carter left office and was opened to the public on his 62nd birthday, October 1, 1986. The research room was opened later in 1987, but not all of the library's collection is available for research as it is still being preserved, arranged, and reviewed for restrictions.

The library's collection is extensive. With more than 40,000 objects that relate to the Carter administration, visitors can get a close-up look at the life of an American president. Within the library's audiovisual collection, there are about 600,000 photo negatives, 1,500 videotapes, and 3,700 audiotapes.

Within the Jimmy Carter Presidential Library and Museum, visitors will find papers and other material relating to the Carter

 ONE-OF-A-KIND TREASURES

administration and the personal lives of Carter and his wife. Among the museum's finer exhibits are Carter's Nobel Peace Prize, a life-size replica of the Oval Office furnished as it was during his presidency, and a walk-through cabin setting of the Camp David meetings. The museum makes use of immersive exhibitions filled with notable objects, documents, photographs, videos, and gifts from world leaders.

Fact BOX

The land that the library and museum sit on was originally slated to be an interstate, a plan which Carter halted when he was governor.

David J. Sencer CDC Museum

For learning how to deal with a public health crisis

Originally established as the Communicable Disease Center and now known as the Centers for Disease Control and Prevention, CDC leads the fight against all infectious diseases. The David J. Sencer CDC Museum is located at CDC Headquarters and is the only part of CDC open to the public. The museum was founded in 1996, coinciding with the 50th anniversary of the Center and the 1996 Summer Olympics. At the time, it was known as the Global Health Odyssey Museum. It wasn't until 2011 that the museum got its new name honoring David Sencer, the longest serving director of CDC, who had passed away that year.

The museum's exhibits focus on the history of CDC and a variety of public health topics, from the complexity of influenza to the ensuring of worker safety. Explore how CDC contributed to the eradication of smallpox—the Center is one of only two labs in the world that

 ONE-OF-A-KIND TREASURES

officially holds the smallpox virus—and learn about the technology required to study infectious diseases (it has one of 15 biosafety level 4 labs in the US necessary to isolate dangerous infectious agents).

The story of CDC and its work in the prevention of infectious diseases is fascinating. Documents, photographs, multi-media installations, and historical objects paint a picture of the Center's accomplishments in public health.

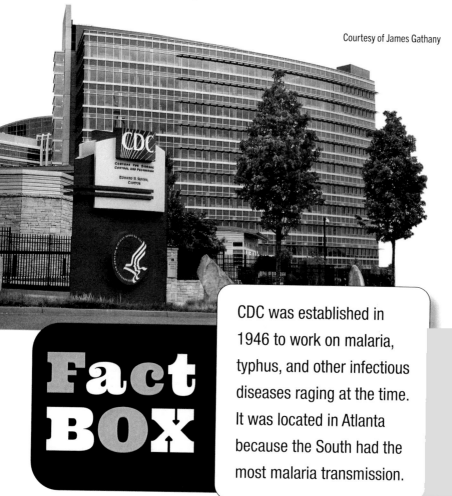

Courtesy of James Gathany

Fact BOX

CDC was established in 1946 to work on malaria, typhus, and other infectious diseases raging at the time. It was located in Atlanta because the South had the most malaria transmission.

Atlanta Street Art

Run-down buildings and dark underpasses get new life from vibrant pieces of art in Atlanta. In recent years, the city has become a haven of street art. Arts conferences like Living Walls, started in 2009, and the OuterSpace Project, started in 2015, champion the mural and street art scene. Meanwhile, Krog Street Tunnel and the Atlanta BeltLine have become hot spots for the city's burgeoning street artists.

The Atlanta BeltLine Eastside Trail is filled with murals from artists like HENSE, Peter Ferrari, and Greg Mike. Krog Street Tunnel has every inch covered in graffiti and street art, and anyone can contribute their own artwork and leave their mark on the town. In Cabbagetown, the annual Forward Warrior public art mural series uses the Wylie Street corridor for its changing array of artwork. In East Atlanta, among the live music venues and retro shops, you'll

 ONE-OF-A-KIND TREASURES

find incredible artwork behind buildings and down side streets from artists like Occasional Superstar and Shaun Thurston.

Street art is everywhere in Atlanta, and each neighborhood has its own gems. In Midtown, you'll find the famous rainbow crosswalk. In Downtown, there's a John Lewis mural by The Loss Prevention. In Little Five Points, look for R. Land's "Pray for ATL." There's always a new mural popping up in Atlanta, and your favorites may be here one day but gone the next.

Fact BOX

The Atlanta Street Art Map (streetartmap.org) has images and mapped locations of over 200 murals and works of street art in Atlanta.

Tiny Doors ATL

What's behind the tiny doors?

All over Atlanta, if you look really closely, you'll be able to find tiny doors tucked away in unlikely spots. These 7-inch door sculptures bring big wonder to a small space. Created by artist Karen Anderson Singer, each tiny door is designed to reflect the spirit or unique element of the community, neighborhood, or institution where the door is located.

The first tiny door Singer installed was on the Krog Street Tunnel in 2014. Since then, Tiny Doors ATL has installed about 25 doors around the city. It has also inspired a movement across the world, and Singer consults with artists to help them bring tiny art projects to their cities. The numbered doors (i.e., Door #1: Krog Street Tunnel) are all free and accessible for anyone to visit. The named doors (i.e., Swan House Door) are located inside Atlanta attractions that you'll have to pay admission to get to.

ONE-OF-A-KIND TREASURES

Tiny Doors ATL inspires pride for the communities and neighborhoods they represent. Singer keeps the doors updated, redesigning and reimagining them when necessary. When a new door is installed, there are Tiny unveiling parties. There have even been Tiny birthday parties for the doors. These doors may be small, but they have grown a huge following—taking a scavenger hunt throughout the city to find all the doors is a great way to see Atlanta.

SIX FLAGS
Over Georgia and
SIX FLAGS
White Water

Atlanta's premier thrill rides and water park

Summer in Atlanta is for amusement parks and water parks. Six Flags Over Georgia, the popular theme park chain, opened west of the city in Austell in 1967. It was the second Six Flags park opened, and with it Six Flags became the first theme park chain in the US. The park's first roller coaster was the Dahlonega Mine Train, which is still in operation today. In 1973, the park added its first wooden roller coaster, the Great American Scream Machine, which was the largest roller coaster in the world at the time. Acrophobia, installed in 2001, was the world's first floorless freefall tower ride. And the park's Riverview Carousel, opened in 1972, is one of three remaining five-abreast carousels in the world.

White Water Atlanta opened as a water park northwest of the city in Marietta in 1984. It came under ownership of Six Flags in 1999 and became Six Flags White Water. It's the only stand-alone Six Flags water park to not use the Hurricane Harbor name. But don't get it

 ONE-OF-A-KIND TREASURES

Courtesy of Larry Felton Johnson, Cobb County Courier on Wikimedia Commons

confused—Hurricane Harbor did open as a section at Six Flags Over Georgia in 2014. When White Water first opened, it had a drop slide, a wave pool, a water slide, and a kid's section. Today, the 69-acre park continues to add new water slides, water coasters, splash area, and raft slides for even more thrills.

Fact BOX

Over 3,000 patrons visited Six Flags Over Georgia on its opening day. Admission cost $3.95 for adults, and parking was only $0.50.

Courtesy of WillMcC on Wikimedia Commons

Stone Mountain

Stone Mountain is just what it sounds like—a small mountain of quartz monzonite located east of the city with a summit of 1,686 feet. Stone Mountain Park, with its 3,200 acres of family-friendly attractions, nature trails, collection of historic buildings, and seasonal festivals, is one of the most-visited attractions in Georgia.

Carved into the side of the mountain is the largest bas-relief sculpture in the world. The carving depicts three Confederate Civil War leaders: president Jefferson Davis, General Robert E. Lee, and General Stonewall Jackson all atop their favorite horses. The sculpture measures 90 feet tall, 190 feet across, and 42 feet deep, and it's positioned 400 feet up the mountain.

 ONE-OF-A-KIND TREASURES

The project was spearheaded by C. Helen Plane, a charter member of the United Daughters of the Confederacy (UDC). Stone Mountain at the time was owned by a Ku Klux Klan member who deeded the north face of the mountain to the UDC in 1916 for the Confederate memorial monument. Sculptor Gutzon Borglum, who would later carve Mount Rushmore, was initially involved in the project and officially began carving the mountain in 1923. After being fired from the project in 1925, his partially-completed carving of Lee's face was blasted off for a new sculptor to begin his work. The carving wasn't completely finished until 1972.

While there has been interest in removing the Confederate monument at Stone Mountain, now owned by the state, a Georgia law that prevents military monuments from being removed or concealed makes this difficult. Stone Mountain Park, meanwhile, has relocated the Confederate flags that previously adorned the base of the mountain, changed its logo to no longer include the carving, and added a new exhibit to address the ugly truth about the monument's history.

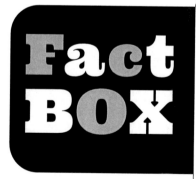

You can hike the 1.3-mile trail to the summit of Stone Mountain, or you can take the Swiss cable car that offers close-up views of the controversial monument.

The Peach Drop

Ringing in the New Year

The Peach Drop is Atlanta's iconic way of ringing in the New Year. This New Year's Eve celebration is traditionally held at Underground Atlanta. Each year, a giant 800-pound peach sculpture made of fiberglass and foam is lowered from its 138-foot-tall tower of lights.

The New Year's tradition began in 1989 with a free all-day festival of food, music, fireworks, and the 58-second drop of the giant peach. The festivities attract huge crowds, anywhere from 60,000 to 170,000 people, and big-name performers like Ludacris, Kansas, Miranda Lambert, Collective Soul, and more.

While preparing for the 25th anniversary of the Peach Drop, a giant yellow M&M appeared on the Peach tower, causing public outcry. Turns out, this was a marketing move by M&M parent company Mars Chocolate who was sponsoring the drop that year. Luckily, the peanut M&M didn't replace the famous peach; instead, the significantly smaller peach made its usual drop in the shadow of the giant candy.

In 2017, with the sale of Underground Atlanta to a private developer, the event moved to Woodruff Park. In 2018, the Peach

FESTIVALS | TRADITIONS

Drop moved back to its traditional place at Underground Atlanta. The Peach Drop's future looked rocky when the 2019-2020 event was canceled in ordered to re-evaluate and expand the event. Then the pandemic put the event on hold for another two years. The Peach Drop finally made its momentous return for 2022-2023.

Courtesy of Rjluna2 on Wikimedia Commons

Fact BOX

The Peach Drop's giant peach weighs 800 pounds and measures 8 feet tall and 8 feet across.

Atlanta PRIDE

The first Pride parade in Atlanta took place in 1970 on the anniversary of the Stonewall uprising in New York City and almost a year after Atlanta's own pivotal Lonesome Cowboys raid. A hundred demonstrators marched in Midtown Atlanta, ending at a rally in Piedmont Park. By 1976, the parade had more than 1,000 demonstrators. Mayor Maynard Jackson declared June 26 to be Gay Pride Day in Atlanta.

Courtesy of Jason Riedy on Flickr

From there, Atlanta Pride grew to more than just a parade and rally. By the 1980s, the days-long celebration included the Hotlanta River Expo, Mr. and Miss Hotlanta Pageants, a live concert, a radio show, an arts show, a film

FESTIVALS | TRADITIONS

festival, a history symposium, multiple parties, competitions, voter registration drive, and open houses for the Atlanta Gay Center and Atlanta Lesbian Feminist Alliance headquarters. The '90s brought an emphasis on public health, a mass commitment ceremony, and the first official Atlanta Black Gay Pride event.

These days, Atlanta Pride isn't held in June, though many events still take place during National Pride Month. In 2009, Atlanta Pride moved its festival, parade, and activities to October, partly because a drought the previous year forced the festival to move from Piedmont Park. In order to get back to the beloved Piedmont Park location, Pride had to work around city policies limiting festivals in the summer. They decided to stick with the October festival to coincide with National Coming Out Day, and the cooler fall weather was better for outdoor events than an Atlanta summer. That just means that Atlantans get two times a year to celebrate Pride: once in June for National Pride Month, and then again in October for Atlanta Pride's festival and parade.

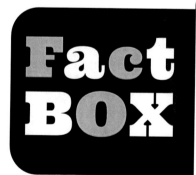

Fact BOX

In August 1969, the Atlanta Police Department raided a screening of *Lonesome Cowboys* at Ansley Mall Mini-Cinema and harassed, photographed, and arrested audience members, spurring Atlanta's first pride parade.

MUSIC Midtown

Atlanta loves its music festivals. And one of the city's favorites is Music Midtown. The two-day festival in Piedmont Park attracts thousands of attendees each year. It has hosted artists like Coldplay, the Black Keys, Pearl Jam, the Foo Fighters, Drake, and Elton John. Even though the festival is well-loved, and had 300,000 attendees at its peak, it hasn't always been an easy show to put on.

Music Midtown began in 1994 as a two-day event at 10th Street and Peachtree Street. Music promoters Alex Cooley, Peter Conlon, and Alex Hoffman wanted the festival to be similar to the New Orleans

FESTIVALS | TRADITIONS

Jazz & Heritage Festival and to present a variety of music. As the festival grew to a three-day event with six main stages, and as Atlanta got redeveloped, Music Midtown was forced to change locations.

Until 2005, it had been held on the first weekend in May. But that year's festival was moved to June to avoid the rainy season. Unfortunately, Tropical Storm Arlene battered the festival. Citing an increase in expenses and lowered attendance, Peter Conlon decided Music Midtown would not return in 2006. The festival remained in hiatus until its return in 2011.

Music Midtown returned for a one-day festival in September 2011 at Piedmont Park with great success, and the next year, the festival brought back its two-day event schedule with three main stages, and a fourth stage was added in 2015. Things were starting to look up for the festival until 2022 when the organizers cancelled Music Midtown in response to Georgia gun laws that prevented the event from banning firearms, since it is held in a public park.

Courtesy of Grant Champagne on Wikimedia Commons

Dragon Con

Where your nerdiest friends will be Labor Day Weekend

Dragon Con was founded in 1987 as a way to welcome all fandoms together into one convention. The founders realized that, while all the conventions focusing on one specialty were great, people have multiple interests and can enjoy many things at once. The convention started as a mix of science fiction and gaming and brought in about 1,200 fans. Add in some rock n' roll, fantasy literature, and special guests, and the attendance started to grow. 1990 was a big year for Dragon Con: they hosted Origins Game Fair '90, one of the largest gaming shows in the country, and they opened the Atlanta Comics Expo. As a multi-genre convention, Dragon Con offers a little something for everyone.

By 2000, attendance had grown to 10,000 people, and the convention organizers officially took Dragon Con from a hobby to a year-round business. In 2001, the convention dates moved to Labor Day and added a parade, and the convention has remained an Atlanta fixture on Labor Day Weekend ever since. At its peak, pre-pandemic levels, Dragon Con was seeing more than 85,000 attendees.

The convention encompasses a five-hotel homebase in downtown Atlanta, taking over the Hyatt Regency Atlanta, the Atlanta Marriott Marquis, the Hilton Atlanta, Sheraton Atlanta Hotel, and the Westin Peachtree Plaza Hotel. Programming has increased to include new

 FESTIVALS | TRADITIONS

Courtesy of Michael Neel on Flickr

areas of gaming, film, robotics, literature, and more. Some of the conventions better-known special guests have included George Takei, Mickey Rooney, James Marsters, Hayden Panettiere, Patrick Stewart, and Stan Lee.

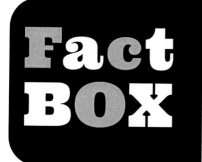

Fact BOX

Dragon Con was so named for the founders' science fiction and gaming group, the Dragon Alliance of Gamers and Role Players.

Peachtree Road Race

A July 4th tradition

Held every year on the Fourth of July, the Peachtree Road Race is a 10-kilometer run and a citywide tradition for professional and amateur runners alike. With a limit of 60,000 spots, the Peachtree Road Race is the world's largest 10k race.

The Peachtree Road Race began in 1970, started by the Atlanta Track Club, with only 110 runners taking the course from the corner of Peachtree Street and Roswell Road to what is now Woodruff Park. By 1978, the race had become so popular that it had to change its course. Now, the race begins on Peachtree Road at Lenox Square Mall and finishes at Piedmont Park at 10th Street and Charles Allen Drive. The first half of the run is largely downhill. Then, runners reach the ¾ mile-long "Cardiac Hill" in front of Piedmont

Courtesy of slgckgc on Flickr

FESTIVALS | TRADITIONS

Hospital. About every half mile, there is course entertainment: DJs, bands, and upbeat playlists motivate the runners.

People come from all over the world to run the Peachtree Road Race. Jeff Galloway was the first winner of the race. The men's course record is 27:01 minutes, set by Rhonex Kipruto in 2019, while the women's record is 30:21, set by Brigid Kosgei also in 2019. Gayle Barron and Lornah Kiplagat have the most victories in the race, with both women finishing in first place five times.

In 1982, the Peachtree Road Race started the Shepherd Center's Wheelchair Division that precedes the foot race and follows the same 10k course.

Atlanta Dogwood Festival

The Atlanta Dogwood Festival is a spring tradition in Midtown, held in Piedmont Park every April. The arts festival features artists and artisans from around the country, musical performances, carnival rides and games for kids, and local food trucks.

The festival began in 1936, the brainchild of Walter Rich, founder of Rich's department stores, who wanted to make Atlanta internationally known for its beautiful blooming dogwood trees. Garden clubs and public citizens planted dogwoods all around the city in preparation for the week-long event. The festival featured pageants, parades, carnivals, and musical performances.

World War II brought an end to the festival for a time, until the Women's Chamber of Commerce (WCC) of Atlanta sparked a renewed interest in 1964. The WCC turned the Atlanta Dogwood Festival into one of the largest civic celebrations in the South. By 1987, the festival

 FESTIVALS | TRADITIONS

Courtesy of Daniel Mayer on Wikimedia Commons

was a month-long event with 30 to 50 smaller events ranging from art shows to hot air balloon races to big-name musicians. In the early 2000s, the event was scaled back to a three-day festival that attracted crowds of more than 200,000 people.

The Atlanta Dogwood Festival stretches throughout the entirety of Piedmont Park. There are over 250 artist booths spread out along the park's walkways, food vendors in a half-dozen different areas, a kids' space, and an international stage with entertainment from more than 20 countries.

Atlanta JAZZ Festival

A month-long celebration of jazz

Maynard Jackson, Atlanta's first African American mayor, created "The Atlanta Free Jazz Festival" in 1978 to celebrate the beauty of jazz and Atlanta's growing reputation as an international center for the arts. Today, the Atlanta Jazz Festival is one of the largest free jazz festivals in the country. The festival is traditionally held in Piedmont Park over Memorial Day Weekend. The three-day festival features a lineup of the best renowned and up-and-coming jazz musicians in the country.

By the mid-2000s, attendance and interest in the festival had grown, so the event expanded to include months-long celebrations of jazz. Beginning in April, you can attend specially curated jazz events throughout Metro Atlanta leading up to the Jazz Fest over Memorial Day. The 31 Days of Jazz event series hosts rooftop concerts, galleries,

 FESTIVALS | TRADITIONS

Courtesy of Mike Flinn on Flickr

and performances at museums and restaurants throughout the month of May. The Neighborhood Jazz Series brings exclusive jazz concerts to communities throughout the city.

Since its start, the Atlanta Jazz Festival has presented jazz aficionados and aspiring musicians a chance to experience a diverse selection of jazz artists from all around the world. Jazz luminaries like Lionel Hampton, Dizzy Gillespie, Ray Charles, and Herbie Hancock have graced the stage of the Atlanta Jazz Festival to bring free entertainment to Piedmont Park.

Georgia Renaissance Festival

A trip back to 16th century England

Located south of Atlanta in Fairburn, the Georgia Renaissance Festival recreates a 16th century English village filled with artisan craft shops, taverns, food stalls, entertainment, and Renaissance-era games. The 32-acre village resembles a Renaissance fair, with a castle façade for the entrance, quaint village shops, and even a jousting stadium. Jugglers, musicians, and storytellers entertain the crowds, while potters, blacksmiths, and woodworkers demonstrate their trade and peddle their wares. Visitors are encouraged to dress up in period clothing or costumes that match the weekend's theme, which can range from pirate to Celtic. If you're in need of appropriate attire, you can buy an entire ensemble from the expert clothiers.

One of the highlights of the Georgia Renaissance Festival is dining on the 1.5-pound turkey leg, a feast fit for royalty. These delicacies are sold at every food court in the village. There is plenty of ale to go around, with a selection of local and domestic brews, ciders, meads, and wines. You can also take a spin on the human-powered carnival

FESTIVALS | TRADITIONS

rides like the Renaissance version of a carousel called the Carasello or the bouncing ride called the Crow's Nest. There are also slides, swings, spinning rides, and more.

The Georgia Renaissance Festival has been around since 1986. The part-circus, part-craft show event takes place over eight weekends from late spring to early summer.

Fact BOX

The Georgia Renaissance Festival grounds have been used as a filming location for *The Walking Dead* and *Loki*.

SweetWater 420 Fest

In 2004, the SweetWater 420 Fest began in the historic Oakhurst neighborhood as a way for SweetWater Brewing Company to celebrate music, beer, and the environment. This Earth Day celebration is a three-day event held on a weekend around Earth Day (April 20). The event brings environmental awareness, features bands from all around the country, and promotes SweetWater's best brews. For years, the festival called Candler Park home, but it 2014 it moved the event to Centennial Olympic Park in the heart of Downtown Atlanta.

While the music and beer are great, environmental awareness is the focus of the event. SweetWater 420 Fest

Courtesy of Shannon McGee on Flickr

 FESTIVALS | TRADITIONS

Courtesy of Shannon McGee on Flickr

has donated more than $120,000 to neighborhood organizations for park improvement initiatives like forming nature paths, restoring pavilions, removing trash, beautifying green spaces, and more. Volunteers and staff even clean the park, pick up trash, garden, and mulch throughout their host park for months after the festival to make sure the park is restored to its original state.

The festival's Planet 420 Eco-Village offers hands-on workshops to educate concert-goers on how to be more eco-friendly. Through the festival's environmentally conscious waste reduction practices, including the use of solely compostable or recyclable materials at all vendor stations, they have diverted 100,000 pounds of landfill waste and created 55,600 pounds of compost waste at the most recent festival.

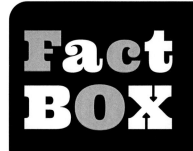

Fact BOX

You can find a solar trash compactor that 420 Fest donated on Broad Street in Downtown Atlanta's popular dining district.

The BLUE CYLINDER in Atlanta's Skyline

Westin Peachtree Plaza

The Westin Peachtree Plaza Hotel is one of the Atlanta skyline's most recognizable buildings. The 73-story hotel stands out with its unique cylindrical shape and reflective blue glass windows. When it opened in 1976 on the site of the old Georgia Governor's Mansion, the Peachtree Plaza Hotel was the tallest building in Atlanta and the world's tallest hotel. It only held the title of world's tallest hotel for a year, but it remained Atlanta's tallest building until 1987.

Designed by Atlanta native John C. Portman Jr., the Downtown Atlanta hotel makes the most of its small site. The 90-foot skylit lobby is laid out around the gigantic core beams that support the tower. At its opening, the lobby originally rose out of an indoor lake known as The Lagoon. In the bar area, "cocktail islands" appeared to float on the lake, and over one hundred trees and cages with live birds added ambiance to the space. Eventually, the lagoon was drained and now it's a fairly standard hotel lobby.

 ARCHITECTURAL MARVELS

Floor-to-ceiling windows give every guest room an incredible view of the city. Though the building appears as a cylinder, each of the 6,350 windows are flat, not convex. On the top floors of the hotel are an upscale restaurant, a cocktail lounge, and an observation level offering panoramic views of Atlanta from 723 feet up. To reach the Sun Dial Restaurant, Bar & View, you'll take scenic glass elevators that go up the outside of the hotel. The Sun Dial Restaurant used to rotate, but after an accident in 2017, the rotation was stopped indefinitely.

Fact BOX

During the 2008 tornado, the Westin Peachtree Plaza sustained damage to over 500 windows. Because the type of window used was no longer made, the hotel had to replace all 6,350 windows over a two-year period.

Atlanta's Flying Saucer

Polaris Restaurant

Polaris, an iconic rotating restaurant located atop the Hyatt Regency hotel in Downtown Atlanta, first opened in 1967. The flying saucer-shaped restaurant and the hotel were designed by architect John C. Portman Jr., the mind behind the Westin Peachtree Plaza. At the time, the Hyatt Regency, with its open-air 22-story atrium topped by the blue-domed restaurant, was the tallest building in Atlanta.

The Polaris became an instant tourist hotspot, which was exactly what the hotel wanted. The idea for a rooftop restaurant was actually an afterthought, a way to get the public more invested and to bring the community to the hotel, even for those not staying there. Then they decided to make the restaurant revolve. The 4,682-square-foot Polaris rotates on a giant turntable that allows patrons to see all of the city.

The showy new restaurant was just the spark that a languishing Downtown Atlanta needed at the time. It was a place to take out-of-town dignitaries, ambassadors, and movie stars. It was also

ARCHITECTURAL MARVELS

one of the first fully integrated Downtown spots—the Hyatt Regency itself was one of the first hotels in Atlanta to welcome black travelers.

In 2004, the restaurant closed for a decade for an extensive renovation, including a redesigned dining room and the installation of a rooftop garden and beehives. The Polaris had to shutter its doors again in 2020 for the pandemic and didn't reopen until the end of 2022. But after each closure, the Polaris roars back to life to an adoring public.

Images courtesy of Connor Carey
on Wikimedia Commons

Fact BOX

After some experimentation with the speed of the restaurant's turntable, at times too slow and at times too fast, the restaurant now makes a full rotation every 45 minutes.

From Shriners to Broadway

The Fox Theatre

The Fox Theatre was built in the late 1920s as the headquarters for Atlanta's Shriners organization. Architect Olivier Vinour took inspiration from the palaces of the Far East, resulting in the ornate mosque-style building. When the elaborate design became too costly for the Shriners organization to keep up with, they sold the building to William Fox, a movie mogul with an empire of "movie palaces" all over the country, and leased part of the building for their "mosque" until 1949. The theater opened on Christmas Day in 1929.

The theater hit a bump during the Great Depression when Fox declared bankruptcy, but by the 1940s it had returned to prominence when its Egyptian Ballroom became the city's most popular dance hall.

But by the 1970s, the theater was in decline again. To save the building from demolition, Atlanta residents created a non-profit called Atlanta Landmarks that launched the "Save The Fox" campaign, raising $3 million toward restoring and reopening the theater. Today, the theater hosts Broadway shows, concerts, and the Atlanta Ballet.

The theater's exterior, auditorium, Grand Salon, mezzanine Gentlemen's Lounge, and lower Ladies' Lounge feature prominent

 ARCHITECTURAL MARVELS

Courtesy of Daniel Mayer
on Wikimedia Commons

Islamic architecture like ablution fountains, arabesques, and minarets. Meanwhile, the Egyptian Ballroom, mezzanine Ladies' Lounge, and lower Gentlemen's Lounge feature Egyptian architecture like tiny sphinxes adorning the makeup tables and a replica of King Tut's throne chair. The 4,665-seat auditorium is set in an outdoor courtyard under an Arabian night sky, complete with flickering stars and passing clouds.

Fact BOX

The Mighty Mo is a four manual, 42-rank pipe organ with 3,622 pipes that was custom built for the Fox in 1929. It's the second-largest theater organ in the US.

The Pencil BUILDING

Bank of America Plaza

Probably Atlanta's most recognizable building is the Bank of America Plaza, affectionately referred to as the Pencil Building due to its dark exterior, lighter open-lattice pyramid, and spire that make the building resemble the writing utensil. The 55-story office building stands 1,023 feet tall, securing its status as Atlanta's tallest building since it was constructed in 1992. It remains the tallest building in the state of Georgia, in the Southeast, and in any US state capital. Bank of America Plaza was built in only 14 months.

Architectural firm Kevin Roche John Dinkeloo and Associates LLC designed the building in a postmodern Art Deco style, reminiscent of the Empire State Building. The 90-foot, 50-ton spire at the top of the building is covered in 23 karat gold leaf. At night, the open-lattice steel pyramid on the top of the building is lit up in a yellow-orange, further adding to its pencil-like appearance.

The office building is positioned on 3.7 acres of land in Midtown, facing its border streets at 45-degree angles to allow for optimal

 ARCHITECTURAL MARVELS

Courtesy of Connor Carey on Wikimedia Commons

views to the north and south. The building's abundance of vertical lines and columns lengthen the look of the skyscraper and also add plenty of corner offices for the tenants working there.

A Work of Art

High Museum of Art

The High Museum of Art was founded in 1905 as the Atlanta Art Association, but it got its new name when the High family donated their home on Peachtree Street to house the museum's collection. The museum moved to a new location adjacent to the original High house in 1955. By the 1970s, the High Museum was ready to expand again.

In 1979, former Coca-Cola president Robert W. Woodruff offered a $7.5 million grant for a new facility that would triple the High's space to 135,000 square feet, and the museum subsequently raised $20 million for the project. The new building was designed by architect Richard Meier, who won the 1984 Pritzker Prize for his work on the museum.

The High's new eye-catching white-enameled building opened in 1983 and resembles a cube with one corner carved out to form the three-story glass atrium at the center of the building. Geometric

ARCHITECTURAL MARVELS

shapes extend from the body of the building, giving it a distinctive, modern design. Inside, curving ramps connect the museum's gallery spaces, drawing inspiration from Frank Lloyd Wright's Guggenheim Museum in New York. The building's design has won many awards, including being named one of the "ten best works of American architecture of the 1980s" by the American Institute of Architects.

The High continued to grow its collection, and that meant more expansion. In 2005, architect Renzo Piano designed three new buildings to more than double the museum's size. The new buildings are simple boxes clad in aluminum panels to align with Meier's white enamel. Piano's design on the Wieland Pavilion and Anne Cox Chambers Wing features 1,000 light scoops that capture natural northern light and filter it into the windowless galleries on the upper floors.

Flatiron Building

Atlanta has its own Flatiron Building, and it's five years older than the one in New York City. Completed in 1897, the 11-story English-American Building was Atlanta's second skyscraper, and is the oldest one still standing.

The building was designed by Bradford Gilbert, a contemporary of the designer of the Flatiron Building's New York sister. Gilbert was known for his work on the world's first steel-framed building and for designing Atlanta's Cotton States and International Exposition. The Flatiron Building was built as a steel-framed skyscraper on a slender, wedge-shaped block between Peachtree Street NE, Poplar Street NW, and Broad Street NW for English-American Loan and Trust Company.

It has retained its exterior Neo-Classical and Neo-Renaissance design and is protected on the National Register of Historic Places. The building attracted an array of tenants, including architects, life insurance agencies, elevator companies, doctors, and lawyers. In recent years, the majority of the 44,000-square-foot building was vacant

ARCHITECTURAL MARVELS

Courtesy of Eohanacht on Wikimedia Commons

except for a few office tenants. In 2015, a developer bought the Flatiron Building and began a $12 million renovation, which involved gutting almost the entire interior due to water damage. In the process, they were able to expose more of the original steelwork, including an original Carnegie-stamped beam. In 2016, the building was reopened as FlatironCity, a "Next Gen Office Space" home to entrepreneurs, startups, a Microsoft Innovation Center, and the Women's Entrepreneurship Institute.

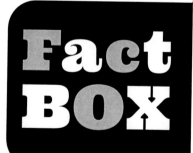

Fact BOX

During the 1996 Summer Olympics, the Flatiron Building was adorned with a giant gold medal, and in 2017, it was the site of the iconic New Year's Eve Peach Drop.

Why is Atlanta so **HOT** and **HUMID?**

While residents don't like the nickname Hotlanta, it is very fitting—Atlanta is undeniably hot. Atlanta is located in a humid subtropical climate, with summers that are hot and humid and winters that are cool and mild. We owe our high humidity to our proximity to large bodies of water and our location in the foothills. Winds passing over the Gulf of Mexico and the Atlantic Ocean bring warm, moist air to the city. The Appalachian Mountains to the north effectively trap the humid air here, resulting in regular rainfall throughout the year and even higher humidity. The average yearly rainfall is actually higher in Atlanta than in notoriously rainy Seattle, even though Atlanta has fewer rainy days.

Atlanta's summers are long, spanning from May through September, with the hottest and most humid month typically being July. The highest temperature recorded in Atlanta was 106 degrees

 WEATHER

Fahrenheit on June 30, 2021. Winter in Atlanta is short and unpredictable, lasting from the end of November through February with the coldest month typically being January. Because hot air can hold more moisture than cool air, Atlanta is able to retain its humidity even into the mild winter. February typically sees the least amount of humid and muggy days.

Fact BOX

The rainiest month ever recorded in Atlanta was July 1994 when Tropical Storm Alberto dumped 17.71 inches of rain on the city, over three times the normal July monthly average.

Why can't Atlanta handle a little SNOW?

On January 28, 2014, a winter storm blew in and crippled the city of Atlanta, stranding motorists for up to 18 hours and sending the city into a state of emergency. With only 2.6 inches of snowfall, the 2014 Snowmageddon left the rest of the country wondering—why can't Atlanta handle a little snow? As those in the South already know, it wasn't just a little snow.

Winter in Atlanta is not typically very cold, with temperatures rarely averaging below freezing. But Atlanta is very wet, and when winter weather hits it's usually a wintery mix, a dangerous combination of rain and snow that then freezes to the roadway, leaving a layer of black ice. In 2014, Snowmageddon froze the interstates and caused 1,200 traffic accidents. Atlanta didn't have the infrastructure in place to combat freezing roadways, like salt reserves or an emergency plan. In response to this disaster, officials more than doubled the amount of salt on hand and created a task force for emergency plans for extreme-weather events.

WEATHER

Courtesy of Stephen Harlan on Flickr

Snowmageddon wasn't the first time Atlanta had been hit by a major snowstorm. A storm on January 23, 1940 brought 8.3 inches, the most snowfall the city has ever seen in a single day. SnowJam 1982 started on January 12, lasted three days, brought between four and six inches of snow, and crippled the city's roadways. In 1993, Atlanta was hit by the Storm of the Century, a cyclonic storm that devastated the East Coast on March 13. The storm had similar pressure to that of a category 3 hurricane, brought 4.2 inches of snow to Atlanta, left 10 million people without power, and killed 318 people across the East Coast. A storm on January 9, 2011 again closed roadways and canceled thousands of flights with less than four inches of snow. While a light flurry isn't uncommon in Atlanta, when snow and ice begin to accumulate, it can lead to catastrophic events.

Fact BOX

The lowest temperature on record in Atlanta was −9 degrees Fahrenheit on February 13, 1899.

Tornados, tropical storms, and hurricanes, oh my!

Winds from the Gulf of Mexico and the Atlantic Ocean do more than just bring humidity to Atlanta; they also stir up some severe weather. Intense thunderstorms and their accompanying flooding are the most common type of natural disaster in Georgia. Summer is thunderstorm season in Atlanta, with most storms occurring in July and August. Storms can trigger flash floods, lightning, and hail damage. In September 2009, Atlanta experienced record-breaking floods from near-constant rainfall, accumulating up to 20 inches of rain in less than 24 hours.

Atlanta is often impacted by tropical storms and hurricanes, even though we're located miles inland. Hurricane season typically

WEATHER

runs from June through November, with the peak in August, September, and October. Since 1950, 29 named storms have come within 100 miles of Atlanta, their impact closing the gap. Damaging winds down

Courtesy of Mark Peppers on Wikimedia Commons

trees and power lines, heavy rainfall that lasts for hours can cause flooding, and tornados can often spawn off tropical systems.

Spring is tornado season in Georgia, typically from March to May with the peak in April, and with tornados typically taking place in the afternoon or early evening. While many severe storm systems coming from the West tend to peter out before they hit the Alabama/ Georgia border, Georgia still sees an average of 26 tornados per year. In 2020, a tornado outbreak over Easter saw 21 confirmed tornados in the Atlanta metro area. In 2008, an EF2 tornado hit Downtown Atlanta on March 14, causing damage to major buildings, killing one person, and injuring 30 others. The tornado damaged the Georgia Dome, which was hosting the SEC men's basketball tournament, and the State Farm Arena, which was hosting an Atlanta Hawks game, and blew the windows out of the Westin Peachtree Plaza Hotel and the Omni Hotel.

Fact BOX

The 2008 tornado is the only time a tornado has hit Downtown Atlanta.

Why is downtown Atlanta **hotter** than other parts of the city?

Atlanta's "heat island"

Some parts of the city are hotter than others. The reason is what's known as the Heat Island Effect, and it's a phenomenon that's not exclusive to Atlanta. A "heat island" is an urban area that experiences higher temperatures than outlying areas. These areas have buildings, roads, and other infrastructure that absorb and re-emit the sun's heat, making daytime temperatures anywhere from 1 to 7 degrees Fahrenheit higher than temperatures in areas with more greenery. Natural elements like trees and bodies of water can help combat heat islands and lower temperatures. Heat islands can happen anywhere where there is little greenery, even in suburban areas, so it's not exactly surprising that Downtown Atlanta would be one.

According to a study by Spelman College and other local institutions, neighborhoods primarily in or south of Downtown have the hottest temperatures. These areas are also mostly historically Black neighborhoods and historically underserved communities.

 **WEATHER**

The easiest way to combat heat islands and cool the city down is to plant trees. Trees and vegetation by provide shade, reflect the sun's energy away from everything in its shelter, and release water vapor through its leaves to cool the surrounding air. Even adding small parks can help reduce the temperature of a neighborhood. The City of Atlanta is using the Spelman College study to help identify which neighborhoods need improvements to help beat the heat.

Fact BOX

Atlanta is recognized as a Tree City by the Arbor Day Foundation for its commitment to caring for community trees and forests.

Hotlanta

If you call Atlanta "Hotlanta," locals immediately know you're not from around here. You'll probably be met with a chorus of "Nobody actually calls it that!" So where did this nickname come from and why does it persist?

The nickname's origins have been hard to trace, but references to "Hotlanta" go back at least to a 1958 column in the Tennessean. A lot of Atlantans remember hearing the term in the '60s. But the name definitely started to take hold thanks to the Allman Brothers Band's instrumental track "Hot 'Lanta," which appeared on their *At Fillmore East* live album in 1971.

"Hotlanta" is a play on words—Atlanta is definitely hot, temperature-wise, and it can be used to describe any of Atlanta's many booming industries from music to sports to business, or just to say that Atlanta is a happening place with plenty to do. The name is used a lot by meteorologists and writers to cleverly get their point across, so it's no surprise that out-of-towners have taken to using the nickname.

But for locals, its use usually elicits an eye roll. Some people hate it more than others, but there are still some with a fondness for

NICKNAMES | PRONUNCIATIONS

"Hotlanta." The general consensus is, you only call it "Hotlanta" when you're talking to people who don't live here, never when talking to locals, at least not un-ironically.

Fact BOX

The Atlanta tourism board has never used "Hotlanta" as an official marketing theme, opting instead for nicknames like The ATL and The A.

At-lan-ta
or At-lan-na

How do you pronounce Atlanta? It doesn't seem that hard, but the proper pronunciation can be divisive—you can typically tell who's from around here and who's not by the way they pronounce the city's name.

Many true native Atlantans tend to pronounce it without any t's, saying it more like ah-LAN-na. Probably the most accepted way, and the way most Southerners would pronounce it, would be dropping at least the last t and saying at-LAN-na. Sometimes you'll hear a bit of a hybrid version with a soft pronunciation of the first t that sounds more like ad-LAN-na. As soon as you pronounce both t's and say at-LAN-ta, you're presumed to be not from around here and likely from the North. Most Atlanta natives find it odd to pronounce the second t at all. You're not likely to be called out for your pronunciation, though, just as long as you don't call it "Hotlanta".

While we're on the subject of proper pronunciations: Dekalb County in the eastern part of Atlanta is pronounced duh-CAB; Ponce de Leon Avenue is not said with the proper Spanish pronunciation but is rather pohnss-duh-LEE-on, and it's perfectly acceptable to just call it Ponce; the northwestern suburb of Smyrna is pronounced SMUR-na; and yes, Cumming is pronounced just like that.

NICKNAMES | PRONUNCIATIONS

Acceptable Nicknames for Atlanta

The ATL, The A, maybe even A-Town

So, if you can't call it "Hotlanta" and locals say you don't pronounce it right, then what can you call this lovely city? Stick to the basics. "The ATL," which is the city's airport code, is a classic—it's easy to say, easy to remember, and hard to mess up. The same goes for "The A," which was popularized by singers and rappers like Ludacris, Lloyd, Lil Scrappy, and T.I. When your city can be identified by only one letter, you've got it pretty good. You could even call it "A-Town," a la Usher and Lil Jon, but that does feel a little too early-2000s.

Atlanta has earned a few other monikers that don't make locals cringe like "Hotlanta" does, though they aren't typically used in casual conversation. You'll probably see Atlanta referred to as a "Black Mecca," the "LGBT Capital of the South," and the "Black Gay Mecca." It's earned the nickname "Silicon Peach" for its rise in tech startups, "Hollywood of the South" for its booming film industry, and "Black Hollywood" for its thriving black entertainment industry. Atlanta is also sometimes called the "City in a Forest" for its lush tree canopy and "Dogwood City" for its dogwood trees.

Hollywood of the South

In 2008, the governor of Georgia signed a generous tax incentive for film productions in order to entice the film industry to the Peach State. The state had just lost the production of *Ray*, a biopic about Georgia native Ray Charles, to Louisiana, and they knew they needed to step up their game. The current incentive gives an income tax credit of 20%, plus an additional 10% for adding Georgia's peach logo to its credits. The state's diverse landscape from city to rural and mountains to beaches appeal to directors. Atlanta can become a stand-in for New York City, a Metro Atlanta suburb can become 1980s Indiana, and a sleepy little town can become overrun by zombies.

At the center of Georgia's film industry is Atlanta, earning the nicknames "Hollywood of the South" and "Black Hollywood". The state's tax incentive attracted films like the *Hunger Games* franchise, Marvel movies, the *Fast and Furious* franchise, and *Baby Driver*. Tyler Perry Studios made its home in Atlanta in 2006 and it has since become one of the largest film studios in the US. Popular television shows like *The Walking Dead, Stranger Things, The Real Housewives of*

NICKNAMES | PRONUNCIATION

Atlanta, and *The Vampire Diaries* have made use of Atlanta's city streets and suburbs. For those that want a look behind the scenes, tours offer exclusive access to filming locations for your favorite TV shows and movies around the city.

Fact BOX

In 2016, there were more major films made in Georgia than in California.

The City in a Forest

Many visitors to Atlanta are surprised to find so much greenery here. Atlanta has a lush tree canopy—one of the highest percentages of overall urban tree canopy in the US at 46.5% (40,609 acres) of the city's total area, according to a 2018 study by the City of Atlanta. The city has about 5,025 square feet of green space per capita, according to Stacker. Even one of the city's most popular festivals, the Atlanta Dogwood Festival, is in honor of trees. It certainly seems that Atlanta loves its trees, and it's earned the nickname of "City in a Forest".

But, like many urban centers, Atlanta is losing its tree canopy and may not be a "city in a forest" for long if things don't change. In 2008, during the city's first urban tree canopy assessment, Atlanta's canopy was estimated at 47.9%. Most of the canopy lost during those 10 years was in the northern parts of the city due to single-family redevelopment, followed by construction of new developments. Any regrowth that the 2018 study saw was of forests on lands that had

NICKNAMES | PRONUNCIATIONS

been cleared for development but left undeveloped, and is likely only temporary. Canopy loss is outpacing canopy gain, and Atlanta is in danger of losing is urban forest.

The City of Atlanta has a long-standing goal for 50% tree canopy coverage. According to the 2018 assessment, the city would need 3,000 more acres of canopy to reach that goal.

Fact BOX

Trees Atlanta was created in 1985 to address the lack of greenspace in the city and has planted 150,000 new trees since its founding.

Atlanta's
Foodie
HIGHWAY

Georgia State Route 13 stretches for almost 50 miles from Midtown Atlanta to Gainesville, but locals know it as Buford Highway. They also know that the best part is the stretch between Buford and Atlanta, particularly just inside the Perimeter, where you can get the best international food in the city.

Before the 1980s, the city of Chamblee, where the majority of this international cuisine is located, was more than 90% white. But when immigrants made their way to Atlanta, they were drawn to the suburbs with its affordable housing, public transportation, and growing construction jobs. The 1996 Olympic Games in particular provided a construction boom that attracted Latino workers, while Asian business owners set up shop thanks to the area's cheap leases. By 2000, Chamblee's population was 65% foreign-born.

This "International Corridor" has more than 1,000 immigrant-owned businesses, more than 100 of which are restaurants. Buford

FOOD

Highway's first ethnic restaurant, the Havana Sandwich Shop, opened in 1976 and is still in operation. Now, there are restaurants representing cuisines from around 20 different countries, including Korean, Mexican, Chinese, Vietnamese, Indian, Bangladeshi, Central American, Somali, and Ethiopian.

At Plaza Fiesta, you'll find food stalls with authentic Latin American cuisine; Pho Dai Loi #2 is probably one of the best-known Vietnamese restaurants in Atlanta; Canton House is the classic place to go for dim sum; at Food Terminal, you can get a mix of Malaysian, Indian, and Chinese cuisines. And after all that dining around, the Buford Highway Farmers Market offers a huge selection of fresh produce and foods from around the world so that you can continue expanding your horizons at home.

Courtesy of Kate Medley

Fact BOX

Buford Highway has one of the most concentrated foreign-born populations in the US.

Soul Food, Famous Fried Chicken, and Civil Rights

Paschal's historic restaurant

In 1947, brothers Robert and James Paschal opened a small, 30-seat lunch counter on what is now Martin Luther King Jr. Drive. The restaurant served only sandwiches and soda and had no stove; Robert had to prepare the food at home and send it by taxi to the restaurant. Their specialty was Robert's own fried chicken sandwich. By 1959, the lunch counter had found great success and moved across the street to a larger building with room for a 90-seat coffee shop and a 125-seat dining room. They expanded their menu to soul food classics like fried chicken, collard greens, and peach cobbler.

Everyone was welcome at Paschal's—the restaurant welcomed both blacks and whites, and disregarded segregation laws. It became the center of the Civil Rights Movement during the 1960s. Civil rights leaders would meet at Paschal's for strategy sessions, with

FOOD

notable patrons like Martin Luther King Jr., Andrew Young, John Lewis, Maynard H. Jackson, Ralph Abernathy, and Fannie Lou Hamer. The Paschal brothers posted bond for arrested protestors and served complimentary meals to those released from jail.

The brothers opened a 125-room motel on the property with the restaurant in 1967, putting up famous guests like MLK, Robert Kennedy, and Jesse Jackson. The restaurant and motel closed in 1996 and the property was sold to Clark Atlanta University.

In 2002, James Paschal and Herman J. Russell opened a modern version of Paschal's Restaurant on Northside Drive in Castleberry Hill. At the new restaurant, you can experience Paschal's famous soul food and Robert's secret fried chicken recipe.

Fact BOX

The Busy Bee Café opened in 1947 just down the street from the original Paschal's, with Mama Lucy Jackson's famous fried chicken also drawing in civil rights leaders.

Turn Right at The Big Chicken

Marietta's favorite roadside landmark

A 56-foot-tall steel-sided red chicken, with eyes and beak that move, stands on the corner of Cobb Parkway and Roswell Road in Marietta. It has long been beloved by Marietta residents, with locals using the landmark for directions—"turn right at The Big Chicken."

The Big Chicken was built in 1963 for a restaurant called Johnny Reb's Chick-Chuck-'N'-Shake. At the time, this part of Cobb Parkway was a newly constructed stretch, and restaurant owner S.R. "Tubby" Davis wanted to take advantage of his prime location with an eye-catching method of advertising. The building was designed by Georgia Tech architectural student Hubert Puckett. Not long after, Davis sold the restaurant to his brother who turned it into a Kentucky Fried Chicken franchise.

KFC has kept the chicken façade, though inside it's just a regular KFC where you can get all your Kentucky-fried favorites. A newspaper

FOOD

clipping displayed inside the restaurant reports that Colonel Sanders himself wanted the building torn down, but relented after learning that this location was the busiest KFC in the world.

After incurring storm damage and years of wear and tear in 1993, KFC considered tearing down the structure, but public outcry saved the chicken—including complaints from pilots who used the building as a reference point when landing. In 2017, The Big Chicken underwent a $2 million renovation, giving the façade a fresh coat of paint, updating the restaurant to KFC's newest design, and incorporating a small gift shop where you can buy Big Chicken paraphernalia from socks to ornaments.

Fact BOX

The original motor that powered the chicken's eyes and beak caused enough vibration to shatter all the windows in the restaurant.

The Dwarf House

In 1946, S. Truett Cathy and his brother Ben opened a diner in Hapeville, near the Atlanta airport, named The Dwarf Grill, which was later renamed The Dwarf House. The tiny diner had only 10 stools and four booths. Here, they developed a pressure-cooked chicken breast sandwich.

The success of The Dwarf House, and the chicken sandwich, led Cathy to open the first Chick-fil-A in 1967 in the Greenbriar Shopping Center food court. Chick-fil-A established its headquarters in College Park in 1984 and opened its first free-standing restaurant in 1986 on North Druid Hills Road.

The original Dwarf House underwent a major renovation in 2021 that expanded the restaurant. The brick façade, stained-glass window, and iconic little red door that you can enter through still remain. The Dwarf House is special because, in addition to the regular Chick-fil-A menu, you can also get classic diner items like Dwarf Burgers, the famous Hot Brown, Mac & Cheese, Fried Okra, and homemade Lemon

Image courtesy of J. Reed on Wikimedia Commons

FOOD

Courtesy of Nicolas Henderson on Wikimedia Commons

Pie. Open six days a week, The Dwarf House offers sit-down, counter, and drive-thru service.

Chick-fil-A has five additional Dwarf House locations around Atlanta that replicate the success of the original. There are also four Truett's Chick-fil-A concepts around Georgia, a Truett's Luau concept in Fayetteville, and three Truett's Grill concepts in the state, all of which aim to offer a unique experience with expanded menu options and sit-down service alongside Chick-fil-A classics.

Fact BOX

After working seven days a week in 24-hour restaurants, Truett decided Chick-fil-A would always be closed on Sunday so he and his employees could rest, and worship if they chose.

Get Sucked into
The Vortex

A quirky bar with killer burgers

Courtesy of Rachel Chapdelaine on Flickr

Opened by three siblings in 1992, The Vortex Bar and Grill is a self-professed "idiot-free zone" where anyone is welcome as long as you're over 21 and can play nice with others. Both the original location in Midtown and the second location in Little Five Points are decked out with kooky and raunchy decorations (hence the strict 21+ policy). The Little Five Points location, opened in 1996, is an Atlanta landmark with its 20-foot "Laughing Skull" façade over the front door.

The Vortex is known for having some of the best burgers in Atlanta. Their claim to fame is the Single Bypass burger, which comes with two bacon grilled cheese sandwiches, four slices of bread, an

 FOOD

8-ounce sirloin patty, 10 slices of American cheese, 9 strips of bacon, one fried egg, and 4 ounces of mayonnaise. It's ridiculously massive and undeniably delicious. You can get it as a Double, Triple, or Quadruple if you feel the need to up the amount of ingredients. As they put it, "Everything we offer is bad for you."

If you're not in the mood for a Bypass, they have other burgers that are still made with big, fat half-pound patties of 100% premium ground sirloin. Try out burgers like the ham-and-pineapple topped Freaky Tiki or the Ka'mana Wa'na Lei'ya with chipotle cream cheese, bacon, and spice pineapple jalapeno jelly.

Dinner at The Vortex is a great time, just remember to leave the kids and the attitude at home.

"What'll ya have?!"

When you walk into The Varsity, don't be alarmed when all the workers start yelling "What'll ya have?!" at you. This overwhelming experience is all a part of the restaurant's charm.

This iconic Atlanta restaurant is the largest drive-in fast food restaurant in the world. But you don't have to drive in if you don't want to—you have the option to drive in, drive thru, or sit in. The Varsity opened in 1928 in a 14-by-35 brick building with a six-stool counter and walk-up window. Frank Grody, the owner, wanted to capitalize on the foot traffic from a trolley stop at Peachtree Street and North Avenue. He named his restaurant "The Varsity" with the hope of expanding to college campuses around the country—the original is just steps away from his alma mater Georgia Tech.

Courtesy of Carol M. Highsmith,
Library of Congress

FOOD

The Varsity claimed the title of "The World's Largest Drive-In" by 1950. Young workers all wanted to be a carhop at The Varsity. "Flossie Mae," a flamboyant carhop whose real name was John Wesley Raiford, was one of the restaurant's most popular carhops in the 1930s and '40s. Carhop Number 46, otherwise known as entertainer Julius "Nipsey" Russell, began working in 1948 and used his time at The Varsity to develop his comedy skills.

If you go to The Varsity, you'll need to know the lingo, which was created as a way to speed up the ordering process. A "naked dog" is a plain hot dog, but a "hot dog" is a hot dog with chili and mustard; a "glorified steak" is a hamburger with mayo, lettuce, and tomato; an "F.O." is a frosted orange shake; "walk a dog" is a hot dog to go, and the list goes on. The Varsity has a list on their website to help you learn the lingo.

Fact BOX

On its first day of business, The Varsity made $47.30 selling hot dogs for just $0.05 each and with the most expensive item on the menu costing only $0.10.

Southern Food and Southern Hospitality

A taste of Southern comfort at Mary Mac's Tea Room

In the early 20th century, American tea rooms were a woman's way into restaurant ownership. Tea rooms were truly a woman's space—the small independent restaurants were owned by women, staffed by women, because no man would work for a woman, and patronized by women. By the 1940s, "tea rooms" had little to do with serving tea and were in fact full-fledged restaurants. Still, it was unseemly for a woman to open a restaurant, so when Mary MacKenzie decided to open up her own restaurant in 1945, she kept with tradition and called it a "tea room." At the time, Atlanta had at least 16 other "tea rooms" around town.

Image courtesy of Gatorfan252525 on Wikimedia Commons

FOOD

Mary Mac's Tea Room opened with a single dining room that seated 75. Though the restaurant has expanded to a 13,000-square-foot building and six dining rooms, the kitchen still operates as it did in 1945 under Mary MacKenzie's order.

The menu and the recipes haven't changed since opening. You'll still get amazing comfort food made with fresh green beans snapped by hand, old fashioned banana pudding and Georgia peach cobbler baked in-house, and the best brewed sweet tea. For first timers, Mary Mac's still brings out a bowl of pot likker (the broth that's left over after cooking collard greens) and cracklin' cornbread (cornbread with crispy pork skins baked into it).

As one of the best places to get Southern comfort food in the city, Mary Mac's is almost always crowded, but it's definitely worth the wait.

Fact BOX

In 1962, Mary MacKenzie handed the restaurant over to Margaret Lupo who desegregated the dining room.

Chicken Salad for Ladies' Luncheons

Hunger Games fans will recognize the Swan House at the Atlanta History Center as President Snow's mansion. But go around to the back of the property, and you'll find a classic Southern luncheon destination for grandmothers, mothers, and daughters. The Swan Coach House used to house the carriages for the Swan House mansion, owned by Edward Inman and built in 1928. The Inman family lived in the house until 1965 when the estate was then given over to the Atlanta Historical Society.

Around the same time, twelve community-minded women and patrons of the arts founded The Forward Arts Foundation. They renovated the carriage house into a restaurant and gift shop in 1967, and later opened an art gallery.

FOOD

The Swan Coach House has a full menu with seasonal items, but most who visit want a traditional luncheon experience and their signature plate, The Swan's Favorite. This dish comes with two scoops of the Swan Coach House's famous chicken salad inside heart-shaped cones, a salad, a slice of frozen fruit salad, and their famous cheese straws (which you can also purchase a bag of in the gift shop). To drink, they have a variety of classic brunch cocktails, their non-alcoholic Swan House Punch, and of course plenty of sweet tea. And for dessert, the Silk Pie is the favorite: chocolate mousse topped with meringue, whipped cream, and shaved almonds, served in a shape that resembles a swan.

All-Day Breakfast, Smothered and Covered

The rise of Waffle House

Neighbors Joe Rogers Sr. and Tom Forkner opened the first Waffle House in Atlanta's Avondale Estates in 1955. The concept combined fast food with table service and 24-hour service. When it opened, there was only one other restaurant in Atlanta that was open 24 hours. They painted their sign yellow to attract passing motorists, and they chose a name based off the highest profit item on their 16-item menu: waffles.

The success of Waffle House seems to lie in its basic menu that has hardly changed since its opening. Couple that with the fact that you can order any item on the menu at any time of day, and that every Waffle House is open 24 hours, 365 days a year, and you've got a winning concept. The menu uses the chain's own diner lingo: "scattered" for spread on the grill, "smothered" is with onions, "covered" is with cheese,

Image courtesy of Bob B. Brown on Flickr

FOOD

"chunked" is with chunks of grilled hickory smoked ham, and "all the way" is with every topping available. Waffle House claims to be the world's leading seller of waffles, ham, pork chops, grits, and T-bone steaks, and says that it buys about 2% of all eggs in the US annually. They also claim that there are more than a million possible hashbrown combinations, but the AJC has calculated only 768.

You can still visit the original Waffle House location, though it no longer serves food. It's now a museum dedicated to the history of the chain. You can sit inside the vintage restaurant, just as you would have in 1955. The museum holds everything from Joe Rogers Sr.'s custom Waffle House blazer to relics salvaged from restaurants destroyed by Hurricane Katrina.

Fact BOX

FEMA uses the unofficial "Waffle House Index" as a measure of disaster recovery based on a Waffle House restaurant's ability to remain open after a severe storm.

The Food Hall Boom

Food halls are a hot culinary trend—picture an elevated version of a mall food court combined with a cafeteria and a community market. They offer a variety of fast-casual dining concepts with high quality food and a gathering place where the community can hang out. With lots of options and communal seating, food halls are a great place for groups of friends to gather.

Atlanta loves its food halls. As of 2022, there are 11 of them spread across the Metro Atlanta area, and at least eight more on the way.

Atlanta's food hall boom started in 2014 with Krog Street Market, a mixed-use development inside an old stove and iron-pan factory, which has a dozen stalls offering foods from pizza to dumplings, a central bar, and a few full-service restaurants. Next came the popular Ponce City Market inside the old Sears Roebuck Building, which contains boutiques, offices, condominiums, and a food hall with everything from gourmet Italian to fresh baked pastries to Indian street food.

Over the years, food halls have thrived in all different parts of Metro Atlanta. Marietta Square Market opened just off the historic Marietta

 FOOD

Square, becoming the first suburban food hall in Atlanta. Ph'east at The Battery specializes in Asian street foods. Then you have Market Hall at Halcyon in Alpharetta, the Collective at Coda in Midtown, Politan Row at Colony Square in Midtown, Chattahoochee Food Works in Underwood Hills, Southern Feed Store in East Atlanta Village, Qommunity in East Atlanta Village, and the Municipal Market at Sweet Auburn Curb Market.

Breweries and
BREWPUBS

Atlanta's craft beer scene

For two decades, between 1972 and 1992, there were no breweries at all in Atlanta. Now it seems like a new brewery opens in the city every day. There are more than 50 breweries and brewpubs in Atlanta, and 155 breweries overall in the state of Georgia.

In 1993, two breweries ended the dry spell in Atlanta: Marthasville Brewing Co., which only lasted until 1997, and Atlanta Brewing Co. (briefly called Red Brick Brewing Co.), which is Atlanta's oldest operating craft brewery. In 1997, Atlanta's most famous brewery came on the scene—SweetWater Brewing. By the 2010s, the craft beer scene in Atlanta was booming with the addition of well-known breweries like Monday Night, Red Hare, New Realm, Orpheus, and Scofflaw.

A few changes in Georgia's strict alcohol laws have helped the craft brewing trend along. In 2004, a new bill ended Georgia's 6% ABV law, allowing you to purchase beers up to 14% ABV. A 2015

 FOOD

bill allowed breweries to sell up to 64 ounces worth of beer to-go in a growler, bomber, or other single container. Probably the best policy change for local brewers was the 2017 bill that allowed breweries to sell directly to consumers rather than exclusively through wholesalers. This meant breweries could offer drinks on-site and no longer had to use the "tour and taste" format. This bill also allowed breweries to host an in-house restaurant, setting the stage for even more growth in the craft beer business.

Sweet
Southern Hospitali- Tea

Sweet tea is an emblem of the South, and it's no different in Atlanta. Even with the city's transplants from all over the world, sweet tea still reigns. The South didn't invent tea, nor did they invent sweetening it, but they did start the trend of adding ice—it is unbearably hot in the South, after all. The earliest known recipe in the US for sweetened ice tea was published in the 1879 *Housekeeping in Old Virginia* cookbook by Marion Cabell Tyree.

Before that, and before the South became a bunch of teetotalers, "tea punch" was all the rage. This blend of tea, sugar, cream, and alcohol was served either hot or cold at social gatherings. By the 1800s, the temperance movement was taking hold in the South and hostesses needed a non-alcoholic version of their tea punch to serve to guests, resulting in just plain sweet tea. With Prohibition making temperance official, sweet tea really took hold. Advancements in electricity and

Image courtesy of Barbara Webb on Pexels

FOOD

Courtesy of Personal Creations on Flickr

refrigeration technology helped make chilled drinks accessible to more people, so people all across the South could enjoy sweet tea in the height of summer.

When ordering at a restaurant in Atlanta, ordering "sweet tea", "iced tea", or just "tea" will likely all result in being served with iced sweet tea. So, if that's not what you want, be sure to be specific.

Fact BOX

The perfect sweet tea recipe is simple: Steep your tea until you have a strong batch, mix in sugar while hot until dissolved, chill your tea in the refrigerator, then serve cold over ice.

Atlanta's Favorite
Drink

Created in 1886 by John Pemberton, Coca-Cola was originally intended to be a medicine and a temperance drink. It was a non-alcoholic version of Pemberton's French Wine Coca. Coca-Cola was named for its ingredients: coca leaves (known for their cocaine compound) and kola nuts (used for their flavor and caffeine). Pemberton said it could cure morphine addiction, indigestion, nerve disorders, headaches, and impotence. In 1888, he sold the ownership rights to Asa Griggs Candler who developed Coca-Cola into the worldwide phenomenon that it is today.

Coca-Cola has become a national icon as well as an Atlanta icon. In a city of Coca-Cola, it's rare (and jarring) to find a restaurant serving

Image courtesy of Wilerson S. Andrade on Wikimedia Commons

FOOD

118

Pepsi. Even though the formula has changed throughout the years, from dropping the cocaine in the coca leaf extract to the failure of New Coke and back to the tried-and-true classic, Atlantans' love of the soft drink company hasn't swayed.

Nearly every major event and attraction in the city is sponsored by Coke. You'll see their advertisements everywhere, including the first wall mural painted in 1894 in Cartersville. In Downtown Atlanta, you can visit the World of Coca-Cola to learn about the company's history, see the vault where the secret formula is reportedly kept, and try hundreds of different Coca-Cola products.

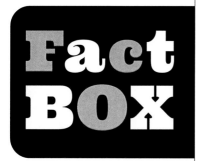

Fact BOX

The first Coca-Cola was sold at Jacob's Pharmacy on May 8, 1886 where it was priced at $0.05 per glass. This fixed price remained until 1959.

Just Peachy

Why the peach still reigns supreme in the Peach State

With more than 70 roads named after peaches, Atlanta is definitely all-in for representing the Peach State. We have the Peach Drop for New Year's, the Peach Bowl for college football, the Peach Pass, and peach license plates.

But the "Peach State" doesn't even produce the most peaches in the US (that's California—Georgia only comes in fourth), nor are peaches Georgia's biggest fruit crop (that would be blueberries).

So why the obsession with peaches? They're really good PR.

Fruit trees were great for replenishing the soil ruined by intensive cotton planting. After the Civil War, the New South needed a new image, one not associated with poverty and slavery like cotton. Town councils latched onto the peach—fruit cultivation was seen as a refined

Image courtesy of Kaolina Grabowska on Pexels

FOOD

activity, and growing peaches required more expertise than cotton. The peach industry blossomed, built on the backs of underpaid African American freedmen. But the face of marketing was the educated farmers and the exotic, delicious fruit.

The peach was named the official state fruit in 1995, and there are nearly 12,000 acres of peaches across Georgia. Peach cobbler is the state's go-to peach treat, and you can find it at comfort food restaurants around Atlanta like Mary Mac's Tea Room and Paschal's.

Courtesy of The Matter of Food on Unsplash

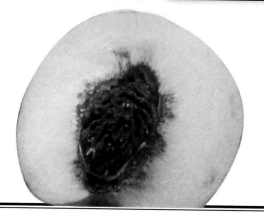

Fact BOX

Calling a woman a "Georgia Peach" originally referred to her light, rosy skin like that of a peach. Now, it generally refers to a woman from Georgia.

Home of the Braves

Not an Atlanta original, but an Atlanta classic

The Braves got their start back in Boston in 1871 when they were known as the Boston Red Stockings. They didn't become the Braves until 1912. After a move from Boston to Milwaukee, the Braves finally came to Atlanta in 1966, and Atlanta has been the "Home of the Braves" ever since.

The Atlanta Braves hit their heyday in the 1990s when they became one of the most successful teams in baseball. The Braves, not having had a winning year since 1983, finished the 1990 season with the worst record in the league but managed to turn it all around in 1991 and make it into the World Series. They lost that World Series but returned for the championship in 1995, 1996, and 1999, winning the 1995 title. From 1991 to 2005, the team won 14

Image courtesy of Jeffrey Hayes on Flickr

 SPORTS

straight division titles and five National League pennants.

Being a Braves fan is full of ups and downs. After a few more disappointing years, the Braves bounced back in 2018 and continued to improve. They returned to the National League Championship Series in 2020 and 2021 and advanced to their first World Series appearance since '99. They won the 2021 World Series, defeating the Houston Astros.

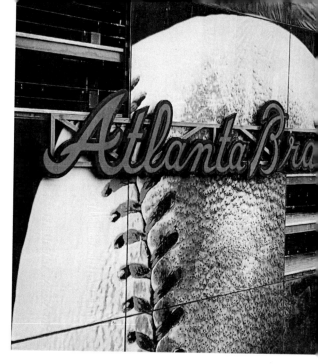

Courtesy of Jon Tyson on Unsplash

Fact BOX

With their start in 1871, the Braves are the oldest continuously operating professional sports franchise in the country.

The Old Home of the Atlanta Braves

HANK AARON HOME RUN

715

April 8, 1974

Turner Field

Courtesy of
Jeffrey Hayes
on Flickr

Located at 755 Hank Aaron Drive, Turner Field was the home of the Atlanta Braves from 1997 to 2016. The stadium was originally built as Centennial Olympic Stadium as the center piece for the 1996 Summer Olympics. After the Olympic Games, the stadium was converted to a ballfield and the Braves made the move from their old Atlanta-Fulton County Stadium across the street.

Atlanta-Fulton County Stadium was demolished after the move and turned into a parking lot for the new stadium. The parking lot was painted with the field configuration of the old ballpark, including a monument section of the outfield wall marking where Hank Aaron's 715th home run went over. While many Atlantans were in favor of naming the new stadium after Hank Aaron, the honor ultimately went to team owner Ted Turner, and the road in front of the stadium was renamed in honor of Hank Aaron and his home run total (755).

 **SPORTS**

Courtesy of David Berkowitz on Flickr

Citing the ballfield's less-than-desirable downtown location, Braves executives opted to move stadiums in 2016. Atlanta's downtown traffic, a shortage of parking, the distance from a MARTA station, and the field's location far from a lot of its fanbase (it was located near some of Atlanta's poorest neighborhoods) all played a part in the move. The Braves played their last game at Turner Field on October 2, 2016. Afterwards, Turner Field was converted into Center Parc Stadium, an open-air stadium for Georgia State University's football team.

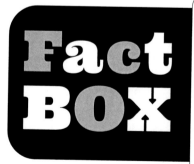

After the Braves's last game at Turner Field, home plate was removed and delivered to their new Cobb County stadium by Hank Aaron and Braves chairman Terry McGuirk.

The New Home of the Atlanta Braves

In 2016, Turner Field was out and the Braves were ready to hit it out of the park with their new stadium SunTrust Park, now Truist Park (this time at 755 Battery Avenue). The new location was considered to be near the geographical center of baseball team's fanbase, and fans now didn't have to brave Downtown Atlanta traffic. The Braves played their first pre-season game at Truist Park on March 31, 2017.

The ballpark's design puts fans closer to the action than they were at Turner Field. Truist Park has a higher percentage of seats in close proximity to the field than any other Major League Baseball park. There is a canopy over the seating and air conditioning at every level to keep fans cool in the hot Georgia summers. On the concourse behind home plate, you can learn about Braves history in the Monument Garden. Memorabilia from the old Ivan Allen Jr. Braves Museum & Hall of Fame at Turner Field has been incorporated throughout the park.

 **SPORTS**

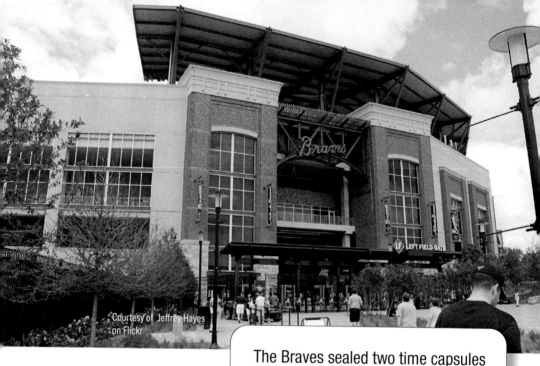

Courtesy of Jeffrey Hayes on Flickr

The Braves sealed two time capsules at Truist Park to be opened when the stadium is demolished. These capsules include parts of the Big Chicken, a 1948 World Series program, dirt from both of the old stadiums, and a baseball signed by the 1995 championship team.

Surrounding the ballpark is an entertainment district called The Battery Atlanta, containing shops, dining, entertainment, apartments, workspaces, and hotels. The Battery provides entertainment all throughout the year, not just on game days. The district is home to a hotel with a rooftop pool overlooking the stadium, the Coca-Cola Roxy music venue, restaurant concepts from some of Atlanta's hottest chefs, and a movie theatre, among others.

Rise Up

Atlanta Falcons

The Atlanta Falcons were established as an NFL franchise on June 30, 1965. Rankin Smith Sr. paid $8.5 million for ownership of the Atlanta Falcons, the highest price ever paid at the time for a franchise. Atlantans were excited to see the new team, and season ticket sales hit 45,000 after a 54-day sale with little promotion, a new NFL record. Unfortunately, the Falcons got off to a rocky start, losing their first nine games of the season.

Since then, the Atlanta Falcons have gone on to win division championships in 1980, 1998, 2004, 2010, 2012, and 2016, and they've appeared in the Super Bowl in 1998 and in 2017.

The team got its name from a 1965 contest. The name "Falcons" was submitted several times. The winner of the contest was Julia Elliott, a school teacher, who described the falcon as "proud and dignified, with great courage and fight. It never drops its prey. It is deadly, and has a great sporting tradition."

The Falcons have had three home stadiums over their career. The first was the Atlanta-Fulton County Stadium, which they shared with

Image courtesy of Keith Allison on Flickr

 **SPORTS**

Courtesy of Georgia National Guard on Flickr

the Atlanta Braves, until 1991. In 1992, the Falcons moved to the newly opened Georgia Dome. And in 2017, they moved to the Mercedes-Benz Stadium, the Georgia Dome's replacement. They were also one of the first teams to have their own year-round practice facility, opened in 1978 in Suwanee and since relocated to Flowery Branch.

Fact BOX

Fans can watch the Atlanta Falcons practice during Falcons Training Camp at the team's headquarters in Flowery Branch.

Mercedes-Benz Stadium

A modern replacement for the Georgia Dome

From 1992 to 2017, Atlanta's home for the Atlanta Falcons NFL team and the Georgia State University Panthers football team was the Georgia Dome. At the time it was built, the Georgia Dome was the second-largest covered stadium in the world by capacity. But in 2010, the Atlanta Falcons wanted to build a new open-air stadium so that the team could play outdoors, and as a bid for hosting another Super Bowl and the FIFA World Cup. At the time, the plan was to retain the Georgia Dome for non-NFL events, but the city decided that maintaining two 70,000-seat stadiums side-by-side was not financially feasible.

Construction on Mercedes-Benz Stadium, as the new open-air venue would be called, began in 2014. The new stadium upgraded the seating capacity to 71,000 total seats, expandable up to 75,000 seats for special events like the Super Bowl, with 7,600 club seats and 190 suites. With 673 concession stands, 24 bars and restaurants, and 1,264 bar taps, Mercedes-Benz Stadium put itself at the forefront of sports entertainment.

 **SPORTS**

Courtesy of Deep-Doshi on Unsplash

Mercedes-Benz Stadium's signature feature is its retractable roof. The roof opens with a pinwheel of eight translucent, triangular panels inspired by the Roman Pantheon. When opened, the roof looks like a falcon's wings extended. When closed, the roof's opacity can be adjusted to control light. Below the roof is the "Halo," a ring of video boards that covers 63,800 square feet around the entire circumference of the stadium. All the electrical systems for the video boards in the stadium are outdoor-rated, so the roof can be kept open even during some precipitation.

Fact BOX

In front of the stadium sits the largest freestanding bird sculpture in the world: the Atlanta Falcon sculpture features a 41-foot-tall falcon with a wingspan of 70 feet perched atop a 13-foot-tall bronze football.

Where College Football Fans Can Get Their Kicks

College Football Hall of Fame

There are plenty of pro football fans, but in the South it's really all about college football. As Hall of Famer Marino Casem put it, "[I]n the South, football is a religion, and Saturday is the holy day."

The College Football Hall of Fame was founded by the National Football Foundation in 1951, but back then it was set at Rutgers University in New Jersey, since Rutgers and Princeton played the first game of intercollegiate football in 1869. The Hall made a few moves, first to Kings Mills, Ohio, then to South Bend, Indiana. In 2009, it was decided the Hall would move to Atlanta and the new museum opened on August 23, 2014.

The football-shaped Chick-fil-A College Football Hall of Fame building sits in Downtown Atlanta's tourism district, bolstered by the

 SPORTS

city's other top attractions. The 50,000 square feet of exhibit space has over 50 interactive displays, a 45-yard indoor football field, and countless football artifacts from your favorite teams in addition to the actual Hall of Fame. You'll see legendary awards like the National Championship Trophy and the Heisman Trophy. You can view in-depth stories and videos on every single player and coach who has ever been inducted into the Hall of Fame. And your whole experience is tailored to you and your team.

The Oldest College Football Field in the South

Though Georgia Tech isn't exactly known for their football prowess, the campus is home to the oldest college football field in the South. The school's Grant Field, named by benefactor and well-known Atlanta businessman John W. Grant for his son, has hosted football games since 1905. It is the oldest continuously used on-campus site for college football in the South and the oldest in the NCAA Division I Football Bowl Subdivision (FBS).

The field didn't get its permanent grandstands until 1913 when they were built mostly by Georgia Tech students. The stadium quickly grew up around the field from the original capacity of about 5,304 to an all-time high of 58,121 in 1968. Subsequent renovations have brought the capacity down to its current 55,000 seats. The old concrete grandstand is still intact underneath the modern renovation.

In 1968, Grant Field hosted the inaugural Peach Bowl and was the venue until 1970. The stadium was renamed in 1988 in honor of Bobby Dodd, the Georgia Tech football coach with the most wins in the team's history. While the stadium bears Bobby Dodd's name, the playing surface is still called Grant Field.

 SPORTS

Bobby Dodd has been the site of more home wins than any other FBS stadium. In 1916, under coach John Heisman, Tech beat Cumberland College 222-0 in the most lopsided game in American football history. In 1928, Georgia Tech played most of its games at home in its regular season due to Grant Field being larger and more accessible than any other stadium in the South at the time. And in 1956, coach Bobby Dodd had what he called his greatest victory when Tech upset top-ranked Alabama and ended their undefeated streak with a 7-6 win. Since 1913, Georgia Tech has had over 480 home wins at Bobby Dodd Stadium.

Fact BOX

Bobby Dodd Stadium has hosted professional football as well. In 1969, the Atlanta Falcons played against the Baltimore Colts there, since the Atlanta Braves were playing in a championship game at their shared Atlanta-Fulton County Stadium.

The Other Football Comes to Atlanta

Before Atlanta United FC, Atlanta was the largest metropolitan area without a Major League Soccer franchise. Atlanta Falcons owner, and co-founder of The Home Depot, Arthur Blank was instrumental in bringing MLS to Atlanta. And the plans for the new Mercedes-Benz Stadium made the city an attractive prospect as well.

Atlanta United was founded on April 16, 2014 and played their first regular season game on March 5, 2017 at Georgia Tech's Bobby Dodd Stadium. Once Mercedes-Benz Stadium opened, Atlanta United made the stadium their new home, sharing it with the Atlanta Falcons.

In its second season, the team won the 2018 MLS Cup, the earliest an expansion team has won the title since 1998. The club has also set records in single-match attendance, season ticket sales, single-season average sales, and total home attendance. The team has gone on to win the 2019 Campeones Cup, the 2019 US Open Cup, and the 2022 eMLS Cup. In 2021, Sportico estimated the club was worth approximately $845 million, the second most valuable club in the league.

In 2017, Atlanta United launched a reserve team, Atlanta United 2, to compete in the United Soccer League. The club also operates a youth academy, officially launched in 2016, that competes in the United States Soccer Development Academy. The academy offers seven

Courtesy of Delta News Hub on Flickr

youth teams by age which are all free for selected players and provides a pathway to create homegrown players for Atlanta United. Atlanta United and Atlanta United 2 have signed 12 players from the academy since its inception.

Fact BOX

In a nod to Atlanta's railroad history, Atlanta United players sign a large golden railroad spike and have a local celebrity hammer it into a platform before each game at Mercedes-Benz Stadium.

Professional Basketball in Atlanta

Atlanta Hawks

The Atlanta Hawks, the city's NBA team, date back to 1946 when they were known as the Buffalo Bisons. After just 13 games, they moved to Moline, Illinois where they became the Tri-Cities Blackhawks, named for Native American leader Black Hawk and the Black Hawk War that took place in the area in 1832. They continued to move around, next to Milwaukee where the team's name was shortened and they became the Milwaukee Hawks, then to St. Louis before finally settling in Atlanta in 1968.

The Atlanta Hawks played at Georgia Tech's Alexander Memorial Coliseum for their first four seasons before moving into the brand-new Omni

Courtesy of Jblee18 on Wikimedia Commons

 **SPORTS**

Courtesy of Hector Alejandro on Flickr

Coliseum, a state-of-the-art downtown arena, in 1972. The Omni Coliseum was demolished in 1997 and replaced with Philips Arena, now called the State Farm Arena.

The Hawks won their only NBA championship in 1958 when they were based in St. Louis. They've only appeared in three other NBA finals, all before coming to Atlanta, in 1957, 1960, and 1961. But since their move to Atlanta, they've been in the playoffs 35 times. Their main rivalries are with the Boston Celtics, who have been their rivals since the team was in St. Louis, and the Orlando Magic.

The Dream Team

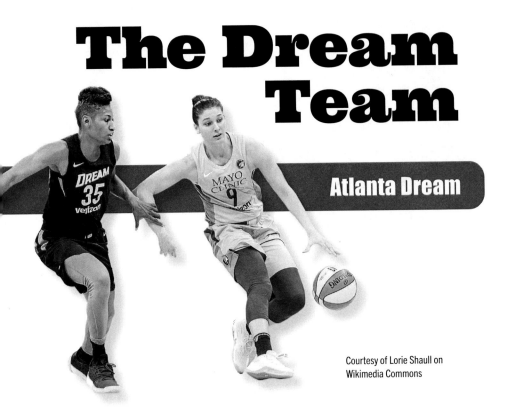

Atlanta Dream

Courtesy of Lorie Shaull on
Wikimedia Commons

The Atlanta Dream is the city's WNBA basketball team, founded in 2008. At the time, the Atlanta Hawks had trouble drawing crowds, so the WNBA was wary about bringing another basketball team to the Atlanta market. After getting over 1,000 petition signatures and pledges for season tickets and bringing Ron Terwilliger on as owner, Atlanta was officially granted a WNBA expansion franchise.

An online poll helped choose the name of the new team, with choices "Dream," "Flight," "Surge," and "Sizzle." The name finally settled on was "Dream," inspired in part by Martin Luther King Jr.'s famous speech. The team's colors were also announced as sky blue, red, and white. The Atlanta Dream played their first season game on May 17, 2008.

 **SPORTS**

Courtesy of Lorie Shaull on Wikimedia Commons

After a rough first season, the Dream went on to make the playoffs in 2009-2014, 2016, and 2018. They've won three conference championships and have made it to the WNBA finals three times.

The Atlanta Dream shared Philips Arena, now State Farm Arena, with the Hawks from 2008 to 2016 with a brief stint at Georgia Tech's McCamish Pavilion while the arena was under renovation. They returned to the renovated State Farm Arena in 2019 but due to disagreement with the Hawks' management, they've elected not to stay. Since the 2020 season, the Atlanta Dream has called Gateway Center Arena in College Park their home.

Sherman's March to the Sea and the Burning of Atlanta

Atlanta's role in the Civil War

Because of Atlanta's status as a railway center and its growing commercial industry, the Confederate Army designated the city as a center for military operations and a main supply route during the Civil War. There were also several hospitals in the city and it was a crucial center for food, ammunition, uniforms, and other military supplies.

After the fall of Vicksburg on July 4, 1863, the Confederates were concerned Atlanta would become a future target. And in May 1864, Union General William T. Sherman began the Atlanta Campaign. By cutting rail lines all around the city, the Union forces were able to cut off the Confederate Army's access to supplies and weaken Atlanta's position. During a five-week siege of the city from July to August, battles took place all around the Metro Atlanta area: the Battle of Atlanta, the Battle of Peachtree Creek, the Battle of Jonesboro, and several others.

On September 1, 1864, Confederate General John Bell Hood evacuated Atlanta and ordered any remaining Confederate ammunition

HISTORICAL INFLUENCE

and supplies destroyed. On September 2, Atlanta Mayor James M. Calhoun surrendered the city of Atlanta to the Union Army. Civilians were evacuated from the city and sent south. The Union Army occupied Atlanta from September 3 through November 16, when they continued Sherman's March to the Sea.

The Burning of Atlanta began on November 12 with the destruction of Atlanta's military assets, all houses used for storage along the railroad, mills, workshops, warehouses, wagon shops, tanneries, and anything that could be considered useful to the Confederate Army. The goal was to destroy Atlanta's, and the Confederacy's, war-making capabilities as well as the will of its people to continue the war. It's estimated that Sherman's army burned about 40% of Atlanta, the majority in the business district around Peachtree Street.

Fact BOX

After the Civil War, the phoenix, the mythical bird that burst in to flames and rises from its own ashes, became a symbol for Atlanta.

The Cradle of the Modern Civil Rights Movement

Atlanta as a beacon of change

Atlanta was a natural choice as one of the main locations for the Civil Rights Movement—the city had a strong community of African American churches, historically black colleges and universities, and local leaders. Dr. Martin Luther King Jr. had grown up here in the Sweet Auburn district, one of the most successful black business communities in the country.

Civil rights leaders like Dr. King, his wife Coretta Scott King, his aids Andrew Young and Ralph David Abernathy Sr., Congressman John Lewis, and others helped Atlanta become a headquarters for the Civil Rights Movement.

King and Abernathy led the Southern Christian Leadership Conference (SCLC), formed in Atlanta in 1957, in training communities and university students in nonviolent protests and voter registration

HISTORICAL INFLUENCE

drives, hallmarks of the Civil Rights Movement. Under their tutelage, student groups organized sit-ins with hundreds of protestors at restaurants around Atlanta to challenge segregation. The SCLC was instrumental in passing the 1964 Civil Rights Act and the 1965 Voting Rights Act.

City officials wanted to keep up with appearances, and Atlanta became "the city too busy to hate", focusing on moving forward in business rather than focusing on past, and ongoing racial tensions. While there were many that still found plenty of time to hate in this busy city, Atlanta did take steps in the right direction. When Ivan Allen Jr. became mayor in 1962, he ordered the removal of all "colored" and "white" signs in City Hall. He was also the only Southern elected official to testify before Congress in support of the 1964 Civil Rights Act.

Martin Luther King Jr.'s Funeral

A 3.5-mile-long goodbye

After Martin Luther King Jr.'s assassination on April 4, 1968 in Memphis, Tennessee, rioting erupted across the country. Surprisingly, Atlanta held to its "city too busy to hate" status and remained peaceful as King was laid to rest five days later in his home town.

There were two services: a private service and a public service. The private service took place first at Ebenezer Baptist Church where 1,300 family members, friends, civil rights leaders, dignitaries, and celebrity figures gathered. The service started with a sermon from Ralph D. Abernathy, King's aid and close friend. King's last sermon, a recording of his "Drum Major Instinct," given on February 4 was played at the funeral. In the speech, he eulogizes himself, telling listeners how he wants to be remembered at his funeral.

HISTORICAL INFLUENCE

Nearly 150,000 people came to Atlanta for the 3.5-mile-long funeral procession that lined the streets of Atlanta from Ebenezer Baptist Church to King's alma mater at Morehouse College where the public service was held. His body was transported in the back of a mule-driven wooden farm cart, one last statement on economic justice. The procession was mostly silent, except for the occasional singing of freedom songs. Morehouse College president Benjamin Mays gave a eulogy and then King was sent to his final resting place at South-View Cemetery, his headstone etched with the words "Free At Last! Free At Last! Thank God Almighty, I'm Free At Last!"

In 1970, King's body was moved to its current location at the plaza between the King Center and Ebenezer, the first steps in building the Martin Luther King Jr. National Historical Park.

Courtesy of Kevin on Flickr

The Largest Concentration of Colleges and Universities in the South

Higher education in Atlanta

The Metro Atlanta area has more than 50 colleges and universities that cover a wide range of disciplines. This gives Atlanta the largest concentration of higher educational facilities in the South.

After the Civil War, Yale graduate Edmund A. Ware founded Atlanta University for Black students—started in 1865, it was the first Historically Black College or University (HBCU) in the South and the first to award bachelor's degrees to African Americans in the South. In 1869, Clark College was founded as the first primarily-black liberal arts college. The two schools consolidated in 1988 to form Clark Atlanta University.

Atlanta University, courtesy of Library of Congress

 HISTORICAL INFLUENCE

Georgia Tech, courtesy of Wikipedia Commons

Along with Morehouse College, Morehouse School of Medicine, and Spelman College, they make up the Atlanta University Center Consortium, the world's largest consortia of African American private institutions of higher education.

Emory University, courtesy of Wikipedia Commons

Georgia Institute of Technology was founded in 1885 as part of Reconstruction plans to build an industrial economy in the post-Civil War South. It started out offering a degree in mechanical engineering, and today Georgia Tech has an emphasis on science and technology and is well-known for its programs in engineering, computer science, and business.

Downtown, Emory University and Georgia State University serve as top research institutes, and Emory Healthcare makes up the largest healthcare system in the state. For liberal arts, Atlanta has Oglethorpe University, Spelman College, SCAD Atlanta, and Agnes Scott College.

The Deadliest Hotel Fire in the US

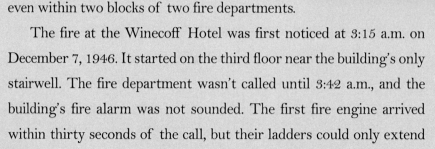

When the Winecoff Hotel (now the Ellis Hotel) opened in 1913, it was one of the tallest buildings in Atlanta and was advertised as "absolutely fireproof." Fifteen stories tall, situated on a lot of almost 4,400 square feet, with about fifteen rooms per floor, the hotel was technically built to code—there was a central fire alarm system manually operated from the front desk, a standpipe with hose racks at each floor, and only one stairway as it was on a lot of less than 5,000 square feet. The hotel was even within two blocks of two fire departments.

The fire at the Winecoff Hotel was first noticed at 3:15 a.m. on December 7, 1946. It started on the third floor near the building's only stairwell. The fire department wasn't called until 3:42 a.m., and the building's fire alarm was not sounded. The first fire engine arrived within thirty seconds of the call, but their ladders could only extend

HISTORICAL INFLUENCE

to the seventh floor. The fire spread slowly up the stairwell but quickly through the hallways, spurred on by the burlap wallcoverings, airflow from the open transom windows between the rooms and hallways, and open windows from guests seeking escape.

The hotel was packed with 285 guests that night. There were 119 casualties, including the hotel's builder and his wife, and 65 injuries. Many people died trying to jump from the higher floors, or fell trying to get to the too-short ladders or using make-shift bedsheet ropes. Others died from the fire itself or from asphyxiation from smoke inhalation.

After the fire, which came only six months after a similar hotel fire in Chicago, a national convention on fire prevention was called. Future regulations addressed issues of combustible building and decorative material, prohibiting operable transom windows in guest rooms, requiring multiple means of exit, requiring sprinkler systems and fire doors, the installation of fire exit maps in hotel rooms, and the enforcement of new standards on older buildings.

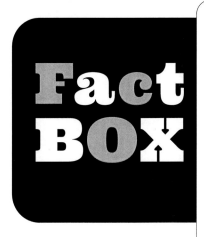

At the time, "fireproof" was a widely-used insurance industry term that only referred to property loss, not loss of life. The Winecoff was deemed "fireproof" in that the building could withstand a fire and return to service without a total building loss.

The Centennial Olympic Games

Atlanta hosts the 1996 Summer Olympics

The fourth Summer Olympics to be held in the United States came to Atlanta from July 19 to August 4, 1996, marking the centennial of the inaugural 1896 Summer Olympics in Athens, Greece. The US did well during the '96 Olympic Games, topping the medal table with a total of 101 medals, winning the most gold medals (44) and the most silver medals (32).

But the Games got off to a rocky start in Atlanta. The city's bid for the Games was a shot in the dark, up against stiff competition like Athens, Greece, and Atlanta was criticized as a "second-tier" city for its Confederate history. However, the city's infrastructure and facilities ranked highly, Atlanta could guarantee large television revenues, and mayor Andrew Young put the spotlight on the city's civil rights history as a "reformed American South." Then, after the Games began, a domestic terrorist set off a pipe bomb at Centennial Olympic Park on July 27, killing two people and injuring 111 more.

 HISTORICAL INFLUENCE

As all Olympic cities do, Atlanta had to develop new venues and infrastructure to accommodate the Games. This included road improvements, developing Centennial Olympic Park, expanding the airport, and improving public transportation. Centennial Olympic Stadium was built for the opening and closing ceremonies and the track and field events, which later became Turner Field used by the Braves. The aquatic facilities and competitor housing were built on the Georgia Tech campus and later used by the university.

Over two million people visited Atlanta for the Olympics, and 3.5 billion people watched from around the world. The 1996 Olympic Games were overall a success that have left a lasting impact on Atlanta. Centennial Olympic Park still has an Olympic Ring fountain to commemorate the games, and the city's Downtown district was revitalized around the park; the Olympic Cauldron can still be seen by the old Turner Field; and an unofficial Olympic Torch, erected by a local real estate developer, stands next to The Varsity overlooking the I-75/I-85 connector.

Fact BOX

The 1996 Summer Olympics mascot was Izzy, originally called Whatizit ("What is it?"), a morphable blue animated character who represents nothing in particular, and at the same time can be anything he sets his mind to.

Image courtesy of Sakhalinio on Wikimedia Commons

Gone with the Wind Which Had Swept through Georgia

Margaret Mitchell

Courtesy of Al Aumuller
on Library of Congress

Margaret Mitchell is one of Atlanta's most famous writers, known for her only published novel *Gone with the Wind*. She was born in 1900 into a prominent and wealthy Atlanta family. In 1925, Mitchell married John Marsh, her second husband, and they made their home at the Crescent Apartments in Midtown, now the Margaret Mitchell House and Museum, which they referred to as "The Dump."

She began her career writing feature articles for the *Atlanta Journal Sunday Magazine*. In 1926, while she was at home recovering from an ankle injury and had read every book she could get her hands on, her husband suggested she write a book of her own. Over the next three years, she worked on her Civil War-era novel, *Gone with the Wind*, which was finally published in 1936. She won the National Book Award for Fiction for Most Distinguished Novel of 1936 and the Pulitzer Prize for Fiction in 1937. The novel was adapted into an award-winning movie in 1939.

FAMOUS PEOPLE

Margaret Mitchell died young, tragically struck by a speeding car as she crossed Peachtree Street with her husband in 1949. She was buried at the historic Oakland Cemetery at the Marsh family grave. Posthumously, she was inducted into the Georgia Newspaper Hall of Fame in 1978, the Georgia Women of Achievement in 1994, and the Georgia Writers Hall of Fame in 2000, and a collection of her teenage writings was published in 1996 as well as a collection of her newspaper articles for the *Atlanta Journal.*

Fact BOX

You can find Margaret Mitchell's grave at Oakland Cemetery, a small collection of memorabilia at the Central Library, and a *Gone with the Wind* Museum in Marietta.

Leader of the Civil Rights Movement

Martin Luther King Jr.

Atlanta-born Martin Luther King Jr. was a social activist and Baptist minister who was a major leader in the American Civil Rights Movement in the 1950s and 1960s. He was born in 1929 and grew up in Atlanta's Sweet Auburn neighborhood, one of the most prosperous African American communities in the country at the time.

He attended Morehouse College at just 15 years old

Courtesy of the Library of Congress

and graduated with a Bachelor of Business in Sociology in 1948. He then went on to attend Crozer Theological Seminary in Pennsylvania

FAMOUS PEOPLE

and earned his Ph.D. in Systematic Theology from Boston University in 1955. In 1957, he helped found the Southern Christian Leadership Conference (SCLC), which aimed to achieve full equality for African Americans through nonviolent protests.

In 1960, King moved back to Atlanta and joined his father as co-pastor of the Ebenezer Baptist Church and continued his work with the SCLC to arrange nonviolent protests, sit-ins, and voter registration drives all across the South. His 1963 March on Washington and work with the SCLC were instrumental in bringing about landmark legislation like the 1964 Civil Rights Act and the 1965 Voting Rights Act. King was awarded the Nobel Peace Prize in 1964 for his work in the Civil Rights Movement, and at the time he was the youngest person ever to receive this award.

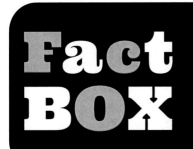

MLK Day was made a federal holiday in 1983, observed the third Monday of January, and was first celebrated in 1986.

Atlanta's First Black Mayor

Maynard Jackson

Maynard Jackson started his career as a lawyer before turning to politics. In 1968, he lost the race for US Senate overall, but he won in Atlanta. He gained prominence in the city and served as Vice Mayor in 1970, the first black person to be elected for the role. After serving four years as Vice Mayor, Jackson was elected as Mayor of Atlanta in 1974 with 60% of the vote. He was the first African American mayor of Atlanta and of any major Southern city.

Courtesy of State Archives of North Carolina on Flickr

FAMOUS PEOPLE

Much of his work as mayor centered around increasing minority businesses in the city, improving race relations, and his public works projects. His upgrades on the Atlanta International Airport's domestic terminal resulted in the airport being renamed for him after his death. As mayor, he oversaw the expansion of MARTA into a rapid-transit rail line, accepted the Olympic flag at the closing of the 1992 ceremonies when Atlanta was selected as the next host city, and oversaw the completion of Freedom Parkway in preparation for the upcoming Olympic Games.

Jackson served three terms as mayor, from 1974 to 1982 and then from 1990 to 1994, making him he second-longest serving mayor of Atlanta, after William B. Hartsfield who served six terms. Maynard Jackson died in 2003 and was laid to rest at Atlanta's historic Oakland Cemetery.

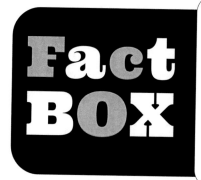

Maynard Jackson graduated high school at the age of 14 and earned his Bachelor's degree in political science and history from Morehouse College at the age of 18.

Putting the Medea in Media

Tyler Perry

Tyler Perry has played a huge role in making Atlanta the "Hollywood of the South" and the "Black Hollywood." Perry came to Atlanta around 1990 where he staged his first play, *I Know I've Been Changed*, at a community theater. By 1998, he had reworked the play and developed a devoted audience of African Americans. From the play's success, he went on to fund his first movie, *Diary of a Mad Black Woman*, and made his directorial debut on his next film, *Madea's Family Reunion*.

In 2006, Perry opened his own film production studio in Atlanta, becoming the second African-American to own a major film studio. Tyle Perry Studios had its first home at what is now Krog Street Market before moving to a location in southwest Atlanta in 2008.

In 2019, the studios moved into 330 acres of the former Fort McPherson army base. The new studio location is one of the largest production facilities in the country with 40 buildings on the National

FAMOUS PEOPLE

Courtesy of Sgt. Michael Connors on Wikimedia Commons

Register of Historic Places, 12 sound stages, 200 acres of greenspace, and a number of permanent sets ranging from a White House replica to a 1950s-style diner.

Perry has been listed as one of *Time*'s most influential people, has been awarded the Governors Award from the Primetime Emmy Awards, has received the Jean Hersholt Humanitarian Award from the Academy Awards, and was inducted into the Black Music & Entertainment Walk of Fame in 2022.

The Center of
Hip-Hop

Atlanta's multi-platinum music artists

Atlanta has a diverse music scene, but it's most known for its hip-hop, rap, and R&B artists. In 2009, the *New York Times* called Atlanta "hip-hop's center of gravity." While hip-hop had a steady rise in the 1980s, it really started to take off in Atlanta in the mid-1990s as the city's artists began developing their own sound different from that of New York City and Los Angeles hip-hop.

Southern hip-hop, Atlanta trap, and crunk music deviated from other styles that largely defined traditional rap music. Atlanta hip-hop artists were able to blend the more laid-back sounds of the West Coast with bass beats from Florida and the hardcore styles of Northern rappers. The synthesizer was integral to creating Atlanta's hip-hop sound and added to the versatility of the music.

When Atlanta-born OutKast accepted their award for New Artist of the Year at the 1995 Source Awards, focus shifted

Courtesy of Sven Mandel on Wikimedia Commons

FAMOUS PEOPLE

Courtesy of MarcoFromHouston.com on Flickr

to Southern hip-hop, and Atlanta in particular. Local record labels like LaFece Records, So So Def Records, and Quality Control Music helped launch Atlanta's hip-hop scene. The city has churned out a number of multi-platinum-selling artists and chart-topping musicians like Ludacris, Ciara, TLC, OutKast, B.o.B., Young Jeezy, T.I., Future, Lil Yachty, Lil Jon, Soulja Boy, and Usher.

Fact BOX

In 2020, there were more than 20 artists with Georgia and Atlanta roots that were nominated for GRAMMYs.

Why Atlanta Can't Have
COX CABLE
Even though They're Headquartered Here

James M. Cox brings his enterprise to Atlanta

Cox Enterprises was founded in 1898 by James M. Cox in Dayton, Ohio when he purchased the *Dayton Daily News*. While in Ohio, Cox was a member of the House of Representatives, Governor, and even the Democratic Party candidate for president, with Franklin D. Roosevelt as his VP, running unsuccessfully against Warren G. Harding in 1920.

After his campaign, he focused on building his media conglomerate, buying up newspapers, radio stations, and television stations around the country. In 1935, he purchased the *Atlanta Journal* and the city's radio station WSB. In 1948, Cox's WSB-TV aired the first television broadcast in Atlanta. In 1950, he purchased the *Atlanta Constitution* (the *Atlanta Journal* and the *Atlanta Constitution* were combined in 1982 to form the *Atlanta Journal-Constitution* or AJC, the city's only major daily newspaper). After the passing of James M. Cox in 1957 and of his son Jim Cox Jr., the company went to James's daughters Anne Cox Chambers and Barbara Cox. In 1982, Cox Enterprises moved its headquarters to Sandy Springs in Atlanta because it was an up-and-

FAMOUS PEOPLE

coming commercial center. Cox launched its high-speed internet in 1996 and its digital cable TV in 1997.

Newcomers to Atlanta often wonder why they can't get Cox internet and cable even though the company is headquartered here. The reason is antitrust laws that prevent a monopoly over media companies–Cox Enterprises already owns an Atlanta newspaper, radio stations, and television stations.

Fact BOX

Before her death in 2020 at age 100, Anne Cox Chambers was one of the richest women in the country, and in 2016 was one of only six women to lead their state in net worth.

Television, Sports, and Bison

Ted Turner

Ted Turner took his father's billboard advertising firm, Turner Advertising Company, and turned it into a prosperous business. In the late 1960s, he turned to buying up Southern radio stations, then sold those to buy a struggling television station in Atlanta. That television station was the start of what would become the Turner Broadcasting System (TBS). When he bought the Atlanta Braves in 1976, he was able to broadcast the games to nearly every home in North America, making the team a household name. In 1977, he bought the Atlanta Hawks in order to provide more TV programming.

In 1980, he launched the first 24-hour news cable channel—Cable News Network (CNN). He bought the film studio MGM/UA, bought World Championship Wrestling (WCW), introduced Turner Network Television (TNT), created the philanthropic Turner Foundation, and

FAMOUS PEOPLE

created the environmental superhero Captain Planet, all before TBS merged with Time Warner in 1996.

Ted Turner purchased a bison ranch in New Mexico in 1996, and now, with about 2 million acres of land, he's the second largest individual landholder in North America. In 2002, the bison rancher founded Ted's Montana Grill, a chain restaurant serving National Bison Association-certified bison burgers, among other things. The restaurant serves as a for-profit effort to stop the extinction of the American bison and has a number of environmentally-friendly policies. The restaurant helped bring back the completely biodegradable paper straw, which hadn't been produced in the US since 1970.

Eat here and we can both live.

Fact BOX

Turner stated that CNN would run "until the end of the world." He even made a video recording of "Nearer, My God, to Thee," as he promised, to be played at the confirmed end of the world.

Making Coca-Cola an International Name

Despite flunking out of both Georgia Tech and Emory University, Robert W. Woodruff went on to turn Coca-Cola into the international phenomenon that it is today. Robert Woodruff and his father, Earnest Woodruff, were part of the group of investors that bought The Coca-Cola Company from Asa Candler in 1919.

Even though Woodruff was doing well as the vice president and general sales manager of White Motor Company, his father offered him the job of president of The Coca-Cola Company in 1923. The Coca-Cola Company was struggling, and Woodruff only intended to bring the price of stock back to what he'd paid for it, sell it, and

FAMOUS PEOPLE

break even before going back to selling cars. Instead, he stayed as president until 1955 and remained on the board of directors until 1984, maintaining control over the company for almost 60 years. In that time, he set high standards for Coca-Cola's quality and service, took the company international by establishing foreign departments, and helped the company weather the Great Depression.

After his work at The Coca-Cola Company, Woodruff dedicated himself to philanthropy. He donated to the Emory University Hospital to establish the Winship Cancer Institute in honor of his mother; to Emory University, with the largest gift ever made to an American educational institution at the time; and to the new Memorial Arts Center, that would become the Woodruff Arts Center. One Robert W. Woodruff Library serves Emory University while another is located in the Atlanta University Center serving Atlanta's HBCUs.

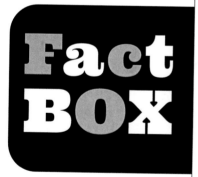

A tribute dinner to Dr. King after winning the Nobel Peace Prize in 1964 was largely unsupported by Atlanta's white business community until Woodruff had Coca-Cola's president and CEO threaten to move their headquarters if the city's business elite didn't step up.

BIBLIOGRAPHY

"5 Things to Know: Surprising Facts about Martin Luther King Jr." National Museum of African American History and Culture. Jan. 30, 2023. https://nmaahc.si.edu/explore/stories/5-things-know-surprising-facts-about-martin-luther-king-jr.

"5 Things You Never Knew about Peachtree Street." *AccessAtlanta*. The Atlanta Journal-Constitution. June 16, 2022. https://www.accessatlanta.com/atlanta-things-to-do/5-things-you-never-knew-about-peachtree-street/VHYC6NW7JRDULEDG6H2BPNDH2U/.

"10 Never before Seen Facts on Truist Park." Sports Teller. July 19, 2022. https://sports-teller.com/10-never-before-seen-facts-on-truist-park/.

"14 Years Ago, a Deadly Tornado Tore through Downtown Atlanta." 11Alive.com. Mar. 14, 2022. https://www.11Alive.com/article/news/local/march-14-downtown-atlanta-tornado-anniversary/85-3476c9f6-ef64-45ab-b73d-0676f6d24e00.

"25 Facts You Never Knew about Coca-Cola." Love Food. Feb. 19, 2022. https://www.lovefood.com/gallerylist/55994/facts-you-never-knew-about-cocacola.

"50 Atlanta Breweries in and around the City." Ramble Atlanta. Dec. 2, 2022. https://rambleatlanta.com/atlanta-breweries/.

"50 Things You Might Not Know about Stone Mountain Park." June 17, 2022. https://www.accessatlanta.com/atlanta-things-to-do/50-things-you-might-not-know-about-stone-mountain-park/ADODVR2I3FHRFKSZA67LMSLTJU/.

Abid, Ayesha. "What's in a Name?: Atlanta." *Georgia Public Broadcasting.* Georgia Public Broadcasting. Aug. 30, 2018. https://www.gpb.org/news/2018/08/30/whats-in-name-atlanta.

"About Peach Drop—New Year's Eve Celebration at Underground Atlanta." *Peach Drop.* Peach Drop. https://peachdrop.com/about.php.

"About Us." Georgia Aquarium. https://www.georgiaaquarium.org/about-us/.

"About Us—the Jimmy Carter Presidential Library and Museum." Jimmy Carter Presidential Library and Museum. https://www.jimmycarterlibrary.gov/about_us.

"About." Zoo Atlanta. https://zooatlanta.org/about/.

Adelson, Andrea. "Seven More Odd Things You Never Knew about College Football Stadiums." ESPN Internet Ventures. Sept. 4, 2015. https://www.espn.com/college-football/story/_/id/13576314/college-football-stadium-oddities-part-two.

Admin. "Delta Air Lines—15 Fun Facts You Must Know about It!" Flyopedia.com. Jan. 3, 2020. https://www.flyopedia.com/blog/delta-air-lines-15-fun-facts-you-must-know-about-it/.

Albright, Mandi. "A Look Back at the Atlanta Tornado of 2008." Mar. 13, 2018. https://www.ajc.com/news/local-govt—politics/look-back-the-atlanta-tornado-2008/s2gWIkY2LOoShXeRmHBVGI/.

Albright, Mandi. "Deja News: 40 Years Ago, Snow Jam '82 Brought Atlanta to a Standstill." Jan. 12, 2022. https://www.ajc.com/news/atlanta-news/deja-news-40-years-ago-snow-jam-82-brought-atlanta-to-a-standstill/KKF7GQIZM5HURBR3IMP3MPINNY/.

Alison. "Inside Dwarf House: Chick-Fil-A's Brand New Massive Diner." *Unofficial Chick-Fil-A Podcast.* ChickfilaPodcast.com. Mar. 11, 2022. https://chickfilapodcast.com/inside-dwarf-house-chick-fil-as-brand-new-massive-diner/.

"An Ideal Worth Protecting." Ted's Montana Grill. https://www.tedsmontanagrill.com/our-story.html.

"Architecture: Atlanta Polaris." Atlanta Expat. 6 Apr. 2018. https://www.atlanta-expat.com/architecture-atlanta-polaris.

"Atlanta 1996 Summer Olympics—Athletes, Medals & Results." International Olympic Committee. June 13, 2022. https://olympics.com/en/olympic-games/atlanta-1996.

"Atlanta an 'Urban Heat Island,' with Higher Temperatures than Surrounding Area, New NASA Study Shows." ScienceDaily. Mar. 25, 1999. https://www.sciencedaily.com/releases/1999/03/990325052848.htm.

"Atlanta Beltline—Bike, Walk, Run or Dine on the Beltline." Discover Atlanta. Aug. 24, 2022. https://discoveratlanta.com/things-to-do/outdoors/beltline/.

"Atlanta Climate, Weather By Month, Average Temperature (Georgia, United States)." Weather Spark. https://weatherspark.com/y/15598/Average-Weather-in-Atlanta-Georgia-United-States-Year-Round.

"Atlanta Dream Team History: Sports Team History." Sports Teams History. May 6, 2022. https://sportsteamhistory.com/atlanta-dream/

Atlanta Dream. WNBA. https://dream.wnba.com/.

"Atlanta." Encyclopædia Britannica, Inc., https://www.britannica.com/place/Atlanta-Georgia.

"Atlanta Falcons Team History." Pro Football Hall of Fame. https://www.profootballhof.com/teams/atlanta-falcons/team-history/.

"Atlanta Hawks Team History: Sports Team History." Sports Teams History. May 3, 2022. https://sportsteamhistory.com/atlanta-hawks/.

"Atlanta Heat Island Study." Scribd. Spelman University and CAPA Strategies. https://www.scribd.com/document/578493214/Atlanta-heat-island-study#.

"Atlanta Hip-Hop Scene—'The South Got Something to Say.'" ChooseATL. https://www.chooseatl.com/live/vibrant-culture/hip-hop.

Atlanta Pride. https://www.atlantapride.org/.

"Atlanta Streetcar Guide—Map, Hours, Fares and Insider Tips." Discover Atlanta. Oct. 1, 2021. https://discoveratlanta.com/explore/transportation/atlanta-streetcar/.

"Atlanta Streetcar." Marta. https://www.itsmarta.com/streetcar.aspx.

"Atlanta United FC Team History: Sports Team History." Sports Team History. May 6, 2022. https://sportsteamhistory.com/atlanta-united-fc/.

"Atlanta University: Lost-Colleges." Lostcolleges.com. https://www.lostcolleges.com/atlanta-university.

"Atlanta's Famed Cyclorama Mural Will Tell the Truth about the Civil War Once Again." Smithsonian Institution. Dec. 1, 2018. https://www.smithsonianmag.com/history/atlanta-famed-cyclorama-tell-truth-civil-war-once-again-180970715/.

"Atlanta's Midfield Terminal Turns 40 Years Old." AirportHistory.org. Nov. 9, 2020. https://www.airporthistory.org/blue-concourse/how-atlantas-midfield-terminal-could-have-looked-completely-different.

"Atlanta's Role in the Civil War." Library of Congress. https://www.americaslibrary.gov/es/ga/es_ga_atlanta_1.html#:~:text=Because%20of%20its%20location%20and,captured%20the%20city%20in%201864.

"Atlanta's 'Spaghetti Junction' Is Still the Worst Bottleneck in Trucking." Fleet Owner. Jan. 25, 2018. https://www.fleetowner.com/news/regulations/article/21701827/atlantas-spaghetti-junction-is-still-the-worst-bottleneck-in-trucking.

"ATL Jazz Fest 2022." Atlanta Jazz Festival. https://atljazzfest.com/.

Atri. "Top 100 Truck Bottlenecks—2023." American Transportation Research Institute. Feb. 8, 2023. https://truckingresearch.org/2023/02/07/top-100-truck-bottlenecks-2023/.

Auchmutey, Jim. "10 Major Moments in History That Shaped the City of Atlanta and Its People." The Atlanta Journal-Constitution. July 27, 2017. https://www.ajc.com/lifestyles/the-top-moments-that-shaped-atlanta/SoZACrBL2mYzbBszhMq3OI/.

Augustyn, Adam. "Atlanta Braves." Encyclopædia Britannica, Inc. Feb. 25, 2023. https://www.britannica.com/topic/Atlanta-Braves.

Augustyn, Adam. "Atlanta Hawks." Encyclopædia Britannica, Inc. Feb. 22, 2023. https://www.britannica.com/topic/Atlanta-Hawks.

Baidya, Johanna. "A City in the Forest: Atlanta's Effort to Preserve Nature in the City: Trees Atlanta." Trees Atlanta. https://www.treesatlanta.org/news/a-city-in-the-forest-atlantas-effort-to-preserve-nature-in-the-city/.

"Bank of America Plaza." Gatech.edu. https://ceelondonblogs.ce.gatech.edu/blog_1/bank-of-america-plaza/.

"Bank of America Plaza." Midtown Alliance. https://www.midtownatl.com/view/bank-of-america-plaza.

Beckham, Jeff. "How the Days Leading up to King's Funeral Played Out in Atlanta." ATL1968. WABE. Apr. 5, 2018, https://mlk.wabe.org/days-leading-kings-funeral-played-atlanta/.

Bentley, Rosalind. "Atlanta's 4-Mile Goodbye to King." The Atlanta-Journal Constitution. Apr. 1, 2018. https://specials.myajc.com/mlk-funeral/.

"Best Atlanta Street Art by Neighborhood." Discover Atlanta. July 19, 2021. https://discoveratlanta.com/stories/arts-culture/best-atlanta-street-art-by-neighborhood/.

"Best Colleges in Atlanta." US News. https://www.usnews.com/best-colleges/rankings/atlanta.

Bevington, Rickey. "What's in a Name?: Spaghetti Junction." Georgia Public Broadcasting. Aug. 8, 2018. https://www.gpb.org/news/2018/08/08/whats-in-name-spaghetti-junction.

Bevington, Rickey, and Emma Burns. "What's in a Name?: Why Everything's Called Peachtree." Georgia Public Broadcasting. Aug. 6, 2018. https://www.gpb.org/news/2018/08/06/whats-in-name-why-everythings-called-peachtree.

Bibb, Porter. *Ted Turner: It Ain't As Easy at Is Looks: A Biography*. London: Virgin Books. 1996.

"The Big Chicken." Marietta. http://www.marietta.com/attractions/the-big-chicken.

"The Big Chicken, Marietta, Georgia." RoadsideAmerica.com. https://www.roadsideamerica.com/story/7021.

"Bobby Dodd Stadium." Georgia Tech Athletics, https://ramblinwreck.com/sports/m-footbl/facilities/bobby-dodd-stadium/.

Brasch, Ben. "Piedmont Park Is More than Selfies, It's Hallowed Music Ground." *The Atlanta Journal-Constitution*. Sept. 13, 2018. https://www.ajc.com/entertainment/music/piedmont-park-more-than-selfies-hallowed-music-ground/QvNSodhE5N6Zczk5DF8LCI/.

"Bringing Big Wonder to Tiny Spaces." Tiny Doors ATL. https://tinydoorsatl.com/.

Brown, Robbie. "Remembering a Soul Food Legend Who Nurtured Civil Rights Leaders." *The New York Times*. Dec. 6, 2008, https://www.nytimes.com/2008/12/06/us/06paschal.html?_r=0.

Burns, Rebecca. "Six Lessons from Riding the Atlanta Streetcar for Eight Weeks." *Atlanta Magazine*. June 12, 2015. https://www.atlantamagazine.com/news-culture-articles/six-lessons-from-riding-the-atlanta-streetcar-for-eight-weeks/.

Butler, Will. "Atlanta Streets: The Complicated Path to Peachtree Street, USA" Atlanta History Center. Jan. 12, 2022. https://www.atlantahistorycenter.com/blog/atlanta-streets-the-complicated-path-to-peachtree-street-usa/.

Capelouto, J. D., and Raisa Habersham. "Peach Drop Moving Back to Underground Atlanta." *The Atlanta Journal-Constitution*. Dec. 19, 2018. https://www.ajc.com/news/just-peach-drop-moving-back-underground-atlanta/0YApA2TJRnUyR97m9uot9O/.

Carlson, Adam. "Remembering Snow Jam 2014." *The Atlanta Journal-Constitution*. Jan. 28, 2021. https://www.ajc.com/weather/remembering-snow-jam-2014-the-numbers/xGVwkyBhoebgNaTAmfGfUO/.

"Catastrophic Atlanta Flood of 2009." NOAA's National Weather Service. Sept. 19, 2019. https://www.weather.gov/ffc/atlanta_floods_anniv.

"The CDC Museum in Atlanta, Georgia." Atlas Obscura. Feb. 24, 2016. https://www.atlasobscura.com/places/cdc-museum.

"Celebrating 50 Years of Atlanta Pride." Edited by Richard L. Eldredge. *Atlanta Magazine*. Oct. 22, 2020. https://www.atlantamagazine.com/atlanta-pride-50/.

"The Centennial Olympic Games: Atlanta in 50 Objects: Exhibitions." Atlanta History Center.Nov. 19, 2020. https://www.atlantahistorycenter.com/exhibitions/atlanta-in-50-objects/the-centennial-olympic-games/.

Chandler, Thom. "Flashback: Snow Jam '82 Rocked Metro Atlanta 40 Years Ago." *The Georgia Sun*. Jan. 13, 2022. https://thegeorgiasun.com/2022/01/12/flashback-snow-jam-82-rocked-metro-atlanta-40-years-ago/.

Chasteen, Deborah. "Yerkes National Primate Research Center." *New Georgia Encyclopedia*. July 14, 2006. https://www.georgiaencyclopedia.org/articles/science-medicine/yerkes-national-primate-research-center/.

Chick-fil-A. (n.d.). Who we are. Chick-fil-A. https://www.chick-fil-a.com/about/who-we-are

Chick-Fil-A Peach Bowl. https://chick-fil-apeachbowl.com/.

"Civil Rights Activism: Atlanta in 50 Objects: Exhibitions." Atlanta History Center. Nov. 19, 2020. https://www.atlantahistorycenter.com/exhibitions/atlanta-in-50-objects/civil-rights-activism/.

Clements, Elaine. "From the History Buzz Archives: It's Time for Tea!" History Buzz. Aug. 22, 2022. https://historybuzz.substack.com/p/from-the-history-buzz-archives-its.

"A Closer Look at the City in the Forest." ArcGIS StoryMaps. July 16, 2021. https://storymaps.arcgis.com/stories/50c3536b558643e98b6fb28eff8dcf9b.

"The Coca-Cola Company." *Encyclopædia Britannica*. Feb. 14, 2023. https://www.britannica.com/topic/The-Coca-Cola-Company.

"Coca-Cola History." https://www.coca-colacompany.com/company/history.

"Colleges in Atlanta." Cappex. https://www.cappex.com/colleges-by-city/colleges-in-atlanta.

Corbett, Suzanne. "Historic Swan Coach House: Lunch for Southern Belles and Hunger Games Fans." Real Food Traveler. Nov. 14, 2016. https://www.realfoodtraveler.com/historic-swan-coach-house-lunch-for-southern-bells-and-hunger-games-fans/.

"Corporate Stats and Facts." *Delta News Hub*. Delta Air Lines. Jan. 6, 2023. https://news.delta.com/corporate-stats-and-facts.

"Cyclorama: The Big Picture: Exhibitions." Atlanta History Center.https://www.atlantahistorycenter.com/exhibitions/cyclorama/.

Danovich, Tove. "The Un-Pretty History of Georgia's Iconic Peach." NPR. July 21, 2017. https://www.npr.org/sections/

thesalt/2017/07/21/537926947/the-un-pretty-history-of-georgias-iconic-peach.

"David J. Sencer CDC Museum." Centers for Disease Control and Prevention. https://www.cdc.gov/museum/index.htm.

Davis, Mark. "150 Years Later, Burning of Atlanta Stands as a Defining Event." *The Atlanta Journal-Constitution.* Nov. 13, 2014. https://www.ajc.com/lifestyles/150-years-later-burning-atlanta-stands-defining-event/zqCN0mtAwGRKGokrYhDaQI/.

Davis, Sebastian. "18 Things You Have to Explain to Out-of-Towners about Atlanta." Thrillist. Apr. 23, 2014, https://www.thrillist.com/entertainment/atlanta/18-things-you-have-to-explain-to-out-of-towners-about-atlanta.

Day, Beth. "Higher Education in the Atlanta Region: Perspectives on History: AHA." *Perspectives on History.* Nov. 1, 2006. https://www.historians.org/research-and-publications/perspectives-on-history/november-2006/higher-education-in-the-atlanta-region.

"Delta First in the *Air." Delta's Firsts in the Airline Industry.* Delta Flight Museum. https://www.deltamuseum.org/exhibits/delta-history/first-in-the-air.

DestinationTea. "The Rise of the American Tea Room: Serving Women's Rights with a Cup of Tea." Destination Tea. Sept. 21, 2016. https://destinationtea.com/the-rise-of-the-american-tea-room-serving-womens-rights-with-a-cup-of-tea/.

Dockterman, Eliana. "How Georgia Became the Hollywood of the South." *Time.* July 26, 2018, https://time.com/longform/hollywood-in-georgia/.

"Dr. Martin Luther King Jr.: Atlanta in 50 Objects: Exhibitions." Atlanta History Center. Nov. 20, 2020, https://www.atlantahistorycenter.com/exhibitions/atlanta-in-50-objects/dr-martin-luther-king-jr/.

"Dwarf House." Chick-Fil-A. https://www.chick-fil-a.com/about/s-truett-cathy-brand-restaurants/dwarf-house.

"Eastern Sub-Continental Divide Mural." Atlas Obscura. Aug. 24, 2020. https://www.atlasobscura.com/places/the-eastern-sub-continental-divide-mural.

Edwards, Christina. "14 Years Ago Today: Looking Back at the 2008 Atlanta Tornado." 95.5 WSB. Mar. 14, 2022. https://www.wsbradio.com/weather/14-years-ago-today-looking-back-2008-atlanta-tornado/NV7FBMSQ5NDHVBWVQSQ6HDHRZY/.

Eldredge, Richard L. "The Polaris Comes Full Circle." *Atlanta Magazine.* July 12, 2018. https://www.atlantamagazine.com/great-reads/the-polaris-comes-full-circle/.

Emerson, Bo. "Atlanta's Winecoff: Deadliest Hotel Fire in US History, 75 Years Later." *The Atlanta Journal-Constitution.* Dec. 3, 2021. https://www.ajc.com/life/atlantas-winecoff-deadliest-hotel-fire-in-us-history-75-years-later/LZUJ3GIRFVGXRFFBOEOMZ7PVRY/.

Emerson, Bo. "Peach to Drop in Peanut's Shadow." *The Atlanta Journal-Constitution.* Dec. 30, 2013. https://www.ajc.com/news/peach-drop-peanut-shadow/hWp16LIps1u1T7v3LQwQFO/.

Estep, Tyler. "Stone Mountain Memorial Association Removes Carving—from Its Logo." *The Atlanta Journal-Constitution.* Aug. 23, 2021. https://www.ajc.com/news/atlanta-news/stone-mountain-memorial-association-removes-carving-from-its-logo/2DEBZPOBSJGN5IVX3TWXSYKBF4/.

"Explore Atlanta's Civil Rights History." Discover Atlanta. Jan. 10, 2023. https://discoveratlanta.com/things-to-do/history/civil-rights/.

Falkenberg-Hull, Eileen. "10 Things You Probably Didn't Know about Georgia Peaches." May 2020. https://www.exploregeorgia.org/things-to-do/blog/10-things-you-probably-didnt-know-about-georgia-peaches.

"Famous Civil Rights Leaders in Atlanta." Discover Atlanta. Jan. 24, 2023. https://discoveratlanta.com/things-to-do/famous-civil-rights-leaders-in-atlanta/.

Figueras, Ligaya. "A Guide to Metro Atlanta Food Halls." *The Atlanta Journal-Constitution.* Apr. 18, 2022. https://www.ajc.com/things-to-do/atlanta-restaurant-blog/a-guide-to-metro-atlanta-food-halls/22NPSDBW6ZH6LLHLR5GHDHWUNA/.

"Flashback Photos: Scenes from Atlanta's Historic 1940 Snowstorm." *The Atlanta Journal-Constitution.* https://www.ajc.com/news/local/flashback-photos-scenes-from-atlanta-historic-1940-snowstorm/kv1Bpk2LyIC7mMF4ZpW18K/.

Flatiron Building. City of Atlanta, GA. https://www.atlantaga.gov/government/departments/city-planning/office-of-design/urban-design-commission/flatiron-building.

Ford, Colleen. "Famous Nicknames Atlanta Holds." AMLI Residential. Jan. 24, 2022. https://www.amli.com/blog/nicknames-for-atlanta-georgia.

"For the Health of the Nation: A History of the CDC in Atlanta." Atlanta History Center. May 7, 2020. https://www.atlantahistorycenter.com/blog/a-history-of-the-cdc-in-atlanta/.

Founding. Delta Flight Museum. https://www.deltamuseum.org/exhibits/delta-history/founding.

Fox Theatre. https://www.foxtheatre.org/.

"Fun Facts—Georgia Aquarium." Georgia Aquarium. https://news.georgiaaquarium.org/internal_redirect/cms.ipressroom.com.s3.amazonaws.com/216/files/20164/Georgia%20Aquarium%20Fun%20Fact%20Infographic.pdf.

Galloway, Jim. "The Cyclorama and an End to a 40-Year Fight over Confederate History." *The Atlanta Journal-Constitution.* July 15, 2015. https://www.ajc.com/news/state—regional-govt—politics/the-cyclorama-and-end-year-fight-over-confederate-history/7qhQVm1jlfTvtGNRGojy5L/.

Gangraw, Sarah. "Sad New Details Revealed about the Death of 5-Year-Old Boy Who Was Crushed at a Rotating Restaurant." YourTango. Nov. 20, 2017. https://www.yourtango.com/2017308597/how-charlie-holt-die-details-boycrushed-revolving-restaurant-parents-sue.

Gatlin, Arielle. "Top Five Winter Storms to Plague Atlanta." WXIA. Jan. 8, 2017. https://www.11Alive.com/article/weather/winter-storm/top-five-winter-storms-to-plague-atlanta/85-382519046.

Georgia Renaissance Festival. https://www.garenfest.com/.

"Georgia's Footsteps of Dr. Martin Luther King Jr. Trail." ExploreGeorgia.org. https://www.exploregeorgia.org/itinerary/georgias-footsteps-of-dr-martin-luther-king-jr-trail.

"Georgia State Capitol." City of Atlanta, GA. https://www.atlantaga.gov/government/departments/city-planning/office-of-design/urban-design-commission/georgia-state-capitol.

"Georgia United States Record High and Low Temperature." Plantmaps.com. https://www.plantmaps.com/en/us/climate/extremes/f/georgia-record-high-low-temperatures.

Gershon, Livia. "The Origins of the CDC." JSTOR DAILY. May 22, 2020. https://daily.jstor.org/the-origins-of-the-cdc/.

Green, Josh. "5 Things to Know about the Recently Renovated Flatiron Building." *Atlanta Magazine.* Sept. 9, 2016. https://www.atlantamagazine.com/news-culture-articles/5-things-know-flatiron/.

Green, Josh. Atlanta Magazine. Apr. 21, 2021. https://www.atlantamagazine.com/news-culture-articles/timeline-evolution-of-the-atlanta-beltline/.

"Guide to Visiting the Carter Presidential Center." *AccessAtlanta.* Sept. 13, 2022. https://www.accessatlanta.com/atlanta-things-to-do/guide-to-visiting-the-carter-presidential-center/CJ6J4CFTHVAJNIWZBUOR6NXWMU/.

Hall, Andrew. "College Football: The Pride and Joy of the South." Bleacher Report. Oct. 3, 2017. https://bleacherreport.com/articles/1875948-college-football-the-pride-and-joy-of-the-south.

Hamilton, Jack. "The Trap: What It Takes to Make It in Hip-Hop's New Capital." *The Atlantic.* Nov. 10, 2022. https://www.theatlantic.com/magazine/archive/2022/11/atlanta-rap-capital-coscarelli-trap-future-migos/671532/.

Hanna, Jason, and Tina Burnside. "Anne Cox Chambers, Media Heiress and Former US Ambassador, Has Died at 100 | CNN Business." CNN. Feb. 3, 2020. https://www.cnn.com/2020/01/31/us/anne-cox-chambers-obituary/index.html.

"Hartsfield-Jackson Atlanta International Airport: Atlanta in 50 Objects: Exhibitions." Atlanta History Center. Nov. 19, 2020, https://www.atlantahistorycenter.com/exhibitions/atlanta-in-50-objects/hartsfield-jackson-atlanta-international-airport/.

"Heat Island Effect." Environmental Protection Agency. https://www.epa.gov/heatislands.

Hicks, Nelson. "6 Things You Didn't Know about the Big Chicken." WSB-TV Channel 2—Atlanta. Feb. 23, 2023. https://www.wsbtv.com/entertainment/things-2-do/6-things-you-didn-t-know-about-the-big-chicken/771508358/.

Hirsh, Ben. "Buckhead Business Spotlight: The Swan Coach House." Nov. 22, 2019. https://www.buckhead.com/the-swan-coach-house/.

"History & Facts." SweetWater 420 Fest. https://sweetwater420fest.com/press/history-facts/.

"History." Atlanta Dogwood Festival. https://dogwood.org/about/history/.

"History." City of Atlanta, GA. https://www.atlantaga.gov/visitors/history.

"History." Cox Enterprises, https://www.coxenterprises.com/about-us/history.

"History of Hartsfield-Jackson Atlanta International Airport." Sunshine Skies. https://www.sunshineskies.com/atl-history.html.

"History of the Atlanta Jazz Festival." https://artsandculture.google.com/story/history-of-the-atlanta-jazz-festival-atlanta-jazz-festival/mgXxKwZsYGbaQA?hl=en.

"History of the High." High Museum of Art. https://high.org/stories/history-of-the-high/.

"History: Peachtree Road Race." Atlanta Track Club. https://www.atlantatrackclub.org/event-information-history.

Hofer, Phyllis. "History of the Atlanta Dogwood Festival." The Atlanta 100. Sept. 14, 2019. https://theatlanta100.com/lifestyle/

living/2018/03/19/atlanta-dogwood-festival-2/15360.

"Home." Atlanta Beltline. https://beltline.org/.

Home: Bank of America Plaza. https://www.bankofamericaplaza.com/.

"Home." BioSidmartin. Mar. 9, 2021. https://biosidmartin.com/why-is-it-humid-in-atlanta/.

"Home." Chick-Fil-A: The Dwarf House. https://www.cfarestaurant.com/hapevilledwarfhouse/home.

"Home." National Center for Civil and Human Rights. https://www.civilandhumanrights.org/.

"Home—Peach Pass: Keep Moving." Peach Pass. https://peachpass.com/.

"How Atlanta Got Its Name." American Name Society. May 4, 2020. https://www.americannamesociety.org/how-atlanta-got-its-name/.

"How Much Longer Can Atlanta Be a City in the Forest?" *Atlanta Magazine.* Dec. 20, 2019. https://www.atlantamagazine.com/list/you-asked-we-answered-34-things-you-probably-dont-know-about-atlanta/how-much-longer-can-atlanta-be-a-city-in-the-forest/.

"How to Ride the Atlanta Streetcar." MARTA GUIDE. Nov. 13, 2019, https://martaguide.com/how-to-ride-the-atlanta-streetcar/.

"International Civil Rights: Walk of Fame: Ivan Allen." US Department of the Interior. https://www.nps.gov/features/malu/feat0002/wof/ivan_allen.htm.

"International Civil Rights: Walk of Fame: Maynard Jackson." US Department of the Interior. https://www.nps.gov/features/malu/feat0002/wof/maynard_jackson.htm.

"Interstate 285 Georgia." Interstate-Guide.com. July 29, 2022. https://www.interstate-guide.com/i-285-ga/.

Jackson, Edwin L. "Georgia State Capitol." *New Georgia Encyclopedia.* https://www.georgiaencyclopedia.org/articles/arts-culture/georgia-state-capitol/.

Johnson, C J. "How Many Food Halls Are in Atlanta?" AtlantaFi.com. Oct. 28, 2022. https://atlantafi.com/atlanta-food-halls/.

Johnson, Craig. "Why Atlanta Is the 'City in a Forest.'" Midtown, GA Patch. Patch. Dec. 27, 2016, https://patch.com/georgia/midtown/why-atlanta-city-forest.

Jordan, Mike. "Your Guide to Atlanta's Buford Highway." *Southern Living.* Aug. 15, 2022. https://www.southernliving.com/travel/georgia/buford-highway.

"June 16 Six Flags Over Georgia Opens." Today in Georgia History. https://www.todayingeorgiahistory.org/tih-georgia-day/six-flags-over-georgia-opens/.

Kahn, Michael. "Rediscovering Atlanta's Architecture: The High Museum." ARTS ATL. July 27, 2017. https://www.artsatl.org/rediscovering-atlantas-architecture-high-museum/.

Kass, Arielle. "Ten Years Later: The Epic 2009 Flood That Submerged Metro Atlanta." *The Atlanta Journal-Constitution.* Sept. 17, 2019. https://www.ajc.com/news/local/ten-years-later-the-epic-2009-flood-that-submerged-metro-atlanta/FwqsjsMsUZXwIQPtnvbHMM/.

Keenan, Sean Richard. "Abundant Green Space Makes Atlanta Nation's 'Most Livable' City, per Research." Curbed Atlanta. July 12, 2019. https://atlanta.curbed.com/2019/7/12/20691567/study-green-space-atlanta-most-livable-city.

Keenan, Sean Richard. "Marta Officially Takes over Atlanta Streetcar Operations." Curbed Atlanta. July 2, 2018. https://atlanta.curbed.com/2018/7/2/17525438/marta-streetcar-downtown-takeover-transit.

Kennedy. "Top 10 Outstanding Facts about High Museum of Art." *Discover Walks Blog.* Sept. 2, 2022. https://www.discoverwalks.com/blog/united-states/top-10-outstanding-facts-about-high-museum-of-art/.

Lada, Brian. "Atlanta and Snowfall: A Rocky History, to Say the Least." AccuWeather. Jan. 14, 2022. https://www.accuweather.com/en/winter-weather/atlanta-and-snowfall-a-rocky-history-to-say-the-least/1124310.

Lambe, Dan, and Lorene Edwards Forkner. *Now Is the Time for Trees.* Timber Press. 2022.

Lambert, Bianca. "Amazing Facts about the Westin Peachtree Plaza Hotel Everyone Should Know." Culture Trip. Dec. 30, 2017. https://theculturetrip.com/north-america/usa/georgia/articles/amazing-facts-about-the-westin-peachtree-plaza-hotel/.

Landsel, David. "A Beginner's Guide to Atlanta's Buford Highway." Food & Wine. Aug. 5, 2022. https://www.foodandwine.com/travel/restaurants/buford-highway-atlanta-best-restaurants.

Lang, Rebecca. "8 Things Only Southerners Know about Tea." Food Network. https://www.foodnetwork.com/recipes/photos/8-things-only-southerners-know-about-sweet-tea.

"Largest Multi-Genre and Pop Culture Convention." Dragon Con. https://www.dragoncon.org/.

Lee, Ra'Niqua. "The Battle of Atlanta: History and Remembrance." Southern Spaces. 30 May

2014. https://southernspaces.org/2014/battle-atlanta-history-and-remembrance/.

Leslie, Katie. "Peach Pass Letter Confuses Commuters." *The Atlanta Journal-Constitution*. May 31, 2011. https://www.ajc.com/news/local/peach-pass-letter-confuses-commuters/MJt9kdHUZyY4c6yYT5gKhN/.

"Margaret Mitchell: American Rebel ~ Biography of Margaret Mitchell." PBS. Mar. 29, 2012. https://www.pbs.org/wnet/americanmasters/margaret-mitchell-american-rebel-biography-of-margaret-mitchell/2043/.

"Margaret Mitchell: Georgia Women of Achievement." Georgia Women. https://www.georgiawomen.org/margaret-mitchell.

"Marta." MARTA. https://www.itsmarta.com/.

"Marta Public Transit Guide—Schedule, Fares & Insider Tips." Discover Atlanta. Dec. 1, 2021. https://discoveratlanta.com/explore/transportation/marta-guide/.

"Martin Luther King Jr: Day, Death, Quotes." *History*. A&E Television Networks. https://www.history.com/topics/black-history/martin-luther-king-jr.

"Martin Luther King Jr. National Historical Park." US National Park Service. US Department of the Interior. https://www.nps.gov/malu/index.htm.

"Martin Luther King Nobel Peace Prize Dinner—News & Articles." The Coca-Cola Company. Jan. 4, 2016. https://www.coca-colacompany.com/news/martin-luther-king-nobel-peace-prize.

"Mary Mac's: Southern Dining." *Mary Macs*. https://marymacs.com/.

"Mary Mac's Tea Room Reopening with New Ownership." Georgia Restaurant Association. Oct. 22, 2020. https://www.garestaurants.org/news/mary-macs-tea-room-reopening-with-new-ownership.

"Maynard Jackson." *Encyclopædia Britannica*. https://www.britannica.com/biography/Maynard-Jackson.

McCoy, Jenny. "A Race Grows in Atlanta: 50 Years of Peachtree." *Runner's World*. June 15, 2019. https://www.runnersworld.com/races-places/a27458332/a-race-grows-in-atlanta-50-years-of-peachtree/.

McCrary, Matt. "Effects of Topography on North Georgia (Atlanta, GA) Severe Weather and Tornadoes." The Weather Prediction. https://www.theweatherprediction.com/weatherpapers/122/index.html.

McGreevy, Nora. "Georgia Approves Changes to Stone Mountain Park, 'Shrine to White Supremacy.'" Smithsonian Institution. Apr. 28, 2021. https://www.smithsonianmag.com/smart-news/georgia-weighs-changes-stone-mountain-park-historic-ku-klux-klan-gathering-place-180977601/.

McKibben, Beth. "Atlanta's Great Food Hall Boom Continues." Eater Atlanta. Oct. 15, 2021. https://atlanta.eater.com/2021/10/15/22728034/food-halls-open-atlanta.

McKibben, Beth. "Downtown Atlanta's Iconic Rotating Restaurant Polaris Finally Reopens." Eater Atlanta. Dec. 7, 2022. https://atlanta.eater.com/2022/12/7/23498438/rotating-restaurant-polaris-hyatt-regency-reopens-downtown-atlanta-2022.

McNair, Charles. "The Dream Center." *Emory Magazine*. Spring 2009. https://www.emory.edu/EMORY_MAGAZINE/2009/spring/center.html.

McQuade, Alec. "What Is Atlanta United's Golden Spike Tradition?" WXIA. Mar. 5, 2017. https://www.11Alive.com/article/sports/what-is-atlanta-uniteds-golden-spike-tradition/85-419935458.

Mellish, Kirk. "Ever Wonder Why So Many Tornado Outbreaks Mostly Skip Georgia?" *95.5 WSB*. Mar. 29, 2022. https://www.wsbradio.com/weather/ever-wonder-why-so-many-tornado-outbreaks-mostly-skip-georgia/WYW4EWHKX5AG7GHCD44CEJAANA/.

Miller, Adrian. "Why Sweet Tea Is the South's Quintessential Drink." First We Feast. June 1, 2018. https://firstwefeast.com/features/2016/07/sweet-tea-quintessential-southern-drink.

Moriarty, Erin. "Turning a Dream into Reality." *Atlanta Business Chronicle*. May 14, 2007. https://www.bizjournals.com/atlanta/stories/2007/05/14/story2.html?page=all.

Moskowitz, Daniel B. "Shocked America Demanded Change after Atlanta Hotel Blaze Killed 119." HistoryNet. May 3, 2020. https://www.historynet.com/shocked-america-demanded-change-after-atlanta-hotel-blaze-killed-119/.

Munsey, Paul, and Corey Suppes, "Turner Field." Ballparks.com.

"Music Midtown." Music Midtown. https://www.musicmidtown.com/.

"National Register of Historic Places Inventory—Nomination Form—Fox Theatre." *Atlanta: National Park Service*. May 15, 1978.

"National Register of Historic Places Inventory—Nomination Form—Underground Atlanta Historic District." *Atlanta: National Park Service*. March 1, 1980.

Newmark, Avery. "5 Flashback Moments from Atlanta's Peach Drop." *The Atlanta Journal-Constitution* Dec. 28, 2021. https://www.ajc.com/things-to-do/atlanta-winter-guide/5-

flashback-moments-from-atlantas-peach-drop/NC5KVD3A2NF6EEAPD5FXMZNGDA/.

Nix, Ramsey. "Saving the City in the Forest." *Atlanta Magazine*. Sept. 28, 2018. https://www.atlantamagazine.com/news-culture-articles/saving-the-city/.

Nord, Melissa. "Here's Why Severe Weather Season Was so Quiet in Metro Atlanta This Year." 11Alive.com. June 5, 2022. https://www.11Alive.com/article/weather/quiet-severe-weather-season-north-georgia/85-7ae05b9f-37e3-48bf-9be3-5637b4017646.

Nord, Melissa. "How North Georgia Is Impacted by Landfalling Tropical Systems." 11Alive.com. May 22, 2022. https://www.11Alive.com/article/weather/north-georgia-hurricane-season/85-3eedffac-ac0e-4b21-b66e-3f35a618eba5.

O'Connell, Rebecca. "11 Late-Night Facts about Waffle House." Mental Floss. Mar. 24, 2021. https://www.mentalfloss.com/article/64018/11-late-night-facts-about-waffle-house.

"On-Line Tour Guide to 1000+ Murals." Atlanta Street Art Map. https://streetartmap.org/.

"Our History—Our Story." Centers for Disease Control and Prevention. https://www.cdc.gov/about/history/index.html.

"Our Story." Waffle House. Dec. 16, 2020. https://www.wafflehouse.com/our-story/.

Parker, Alexandra, and Adam Murphy. "Atlanta's *Music Midtown* 2022 Canceled, Gun Law May Be to Blame." Atlanta News First. Aug. 1, 2022. https://www.atlantanewsfirst.com/2022/08/01/music-midtown-2022-canceled/.

Perez, Dalia. "Atlanta's 'Heat Island:' A Look at Which Parts of the City Are the Hottest and Why." 11Alive.com. June 16, 2022. https://www.11Alive.com/article/tech/science/environment/atanta-heat-islands-where-they-are-study-maps-spelman-university/85-d3c5f9c0-2c36-4e66-9a54-eabbdc652f8b.

Perry, Chuck. "Atlanta Journal-Constitution—New Georgia Encyclopedia." *New Georgia Encyclopedia*. Jan. 5, 2004. https://www.georgiaencyclopedia.org/articles/arts-culture/atlanta-journal-constitution/.

Pete, Joleen. "What You Need to Know about Atlanta's Famous Peachtree Streets." Discover Atlanta. July 15, 2022. https://discoveratlanta.com/stories/things-to-do/what-you-need-to-know-about-atlantas-famous-peachtree-streets/.

Pirani, Fiza. "Waffle House, by the Numbers." *The Atlanta Journal-Constitution* Aug. 13, 2019. https://www.ajc.com/entertainment/dining/waffle-house-the-numbers/nfNge1HkMGFGY1hWgEQwBM/.

Pratt, Timothy, and Rick Rojas. "Giant Confederate Monument Will Remain at Revamped Stone Mountain." *The New York Times*. May 24, 2021. https://www.nytimes.com/2021/05/24/us/stone-mountain-confederate-monument-georgia.html.

Pritchett, Amy R. "Hartsfield-Jackson Atlanta International Airport." *New Georgia Encyclopedia*. Dec. 6, 2002. https://www.georgiaencyclopedia.org/articles/business-economy/hartsfield-jackson-atlanta-international-airport/.

Rankin, Bill. "City of Atlanta Settles Lawsuit with Street Artists." *The Atlanta Journal-Constitution* June 26, 2017. https://www.ajc.com/blog/legal/city-atlanta-settles-lawsuit-with-street-artists/NGx1GmFQ7hKM9JoGnWvFUL/.

Rattenbury, Jack. "Everything You Need to Know about Atlanta Pride Weekend." Secret Atlanta. Oct. 6, 2022. https://secretatlanta.co/atlanta-pride-festival-2022/.

Raymond, Jonathan. "Go Outside and Appreciate the Clear Conditions, Because Six Years Ago Today Was Snowmageddon." 11Alive.com, Jan. 28, 2020, https://www.11Alive.com/article/news/history/atlanta-snowmageddon-2014-anniversary/85-bcf15186-4d02-4a47-8025-5a2cc1f3fdac.

Raymond, Jonathan. "I-285 Turns 50 Years Old Today." 11Alive.com. Oct. 15, 2019. https://www.11Alive.com/article/traffic/i-285-50-years/85-a07aa0b5-c5e1-43bb-8e2e-eeefecf27701.

Reed, Kayla. "Atlanta: Cradle of the Civil Rights Movement." PRsay. Oct. 15, 2015. https://prsay.prsa.org/2015/10/15/atlanta-cradle-of-the-civil-rights-movement/.

"Remember This? 14 Years Ago Today a Tornado Tore through Downtown Atlanta." WSB-TV Channel 2—Atlanta. Mar. 14, 2022. https://www.wsbtv.com/news/local/remember-this-14-years-ago-today-tornado-tore-through-downtown-atlanta/KBKP3A4QDE52CMXDLZK33NCOKY/.

Riley, Betsy. "The (Somewhat Definitive) Ranking of Atlanta's Peachtree Streets." *Atlanta Magazine*. Sept. 19, 2022. https://www.atlantamagazine.com/news-culture-articles/the-somewhat-definitive-ranking-of-atlantas-peachtree-streets/.

Robbins, Chris. "Atlanta's Top 20 Snowstorms & Temperature Trends." IWeatherNet. Feb. 17, 2020. https://www.iweathernet.com/educational/warm-snowstorms-and-atlanta-biggest-snowfalls-on-record.

Roberson, Doug. "How Did Atlanta Become the Center of the College Football Universe?" *The Atlanta Journal-Constitution* Dec. 22, 2022. https://www.ajc.com/sports/georgia-bulldogs/how-did-atlanta-become-the-center-of-the-college-football-universe/YQ3WNYTDANDCTCLKCQR77QA4RI/.

"Robert W. Woodruff Foundation: About. Robert W. Woodruff Foundation. https://woodruff.org/about/robert-w-woodruff/.

Sack, Kevin. "An Era Passes at One Place That Fed the Civil Rights Struggle." *The New York Times.* Apr. 15, 1996. https://www.nytimes.com/1996/04/15/us/an-era-passes-at-one-place-that-fed-the-civil-rights-struggle.html.

Sack, Kevin. "R. H. Paschal, 88, Restaurateur Who Nurtured Rights Leadership." *The New York Times.* Mar. 4, 1997. https://www.nytimes.com/1997/03/04/us/r-h-paschal-88-restaurateur-who-nurtured-rights-leadership.html.

Salas, Erick Burgueño. "Topic: Delta Air Lines." Statista. Sept. 7, 2022. https://www.statista.com/topics/3061/delta-air-lines/.

Saliby, Sophia. "How Atlanta Came to Own the World's Busiest Airport." Georgia Public Broadcasting. 15 Mar. 2019. https://www.gpb.org/news/2019/03/15/how-atlanta-came-own-the-worlds-busiest-airport.

Saporta, Maria. "Atlanta's Urban Tree Canopy Leads the Nation; but Most Trees Are Not Protected." SaportaReport. May 15, 2017. https://saportareport.com/atlantas-urban-tree-canopy-leads-nation-trees-not-protected/columnists/mariasmetro/maria_saporta/.

"Shepherd Center's Wheelchair Division of the Atlanta Journal-Constitution Peachtree Road Race." Shepherd Center. https://www.shepherd.org/patient-programs/sports-recreation/peachtree-road-race.

"Six Flags over Georgia—Thrill Capital of the South." Six Flags. Mar. 1, 2023. https://www.sixflags.com/overgeorgia.

"Six Flags White Water." *Aquatics International.* Jan. 1, 2008. https://www.aquaticsintl.com/awards/six-flags-white-water_0.

"Six Flags White Water: Georgia's Most Thrilling Water Park." Six Flags. https://www.sixflags.com/whitewater.

Smolski, Chet. "Georgia: The Westin Peachtree Plaza, Atlanta." Digital Commons @ RIC. https://digitalcommons.ric.edu/smolski_images/832/.

"So Much More than Doors: What You Don't Know about Tiny Doors Atl." *Atlanta Magazine.* July 31, 2019. https://www.atlantamagazine.com/news-culture-articles/so-much-more-than-doors-what-you-dont-know-about-tiny-doors-atl/.

Southern Kitchen. "Learn How the South Became Synonymous with Sweet Tea." *Southern Kitchen.* Aug. 27, 2021. https://www.southernkitchen.com/story/drink/2021/08/27/learn-how-south-became-synonymous-sweet-tea/5617911001/.

"Spaghetti Junction in Atlanta." *New Georgia Encyclopedia.* https://www.georgiaencyclopedia.org/articles/counties-cities-neighborhoods/atlanta/spaghetti-junction_001/.

Stacker. "Georgia Has 1 of the 50 Cities with the Most Green Space per Capita." Stacker. Jan. 10, 2022. https://stacker.com/georgia/georgia-has-1-50-cities-most-green-space-capita.

"Stadium Fast Facts." Mercedes Benz Stadium. Sept. 19, 2017. https://mercedesbenzstadium.com/stadium-fast-facts/.

Staff, Eater. "35 Atlanta Breweries and Brewpubs to Grab a Pint Today." Eater Atlanta. June 28, 2017. https://atlanta.eater.com/maps/atlanta-hottest-breweries.

"Stone Mountain Park." SStone Mountain Park. https://stonemountainpark.com/.

"Story of the Braves: Atlanta Braves." MLB Advanced Media, LP. https://www.mlb.com/braves/history/story-of-the-braves.

Sugiura, Ken. "Love or Loathe It, City's Nickname Is Accurate for Summer." *The Atlanta Journal-Constitution* June 16, 2008. https://www.ajc.com/atlanta-weather/love-or-loathe-it-citys-nickname-is-accurate-for-summer/UN3SNYM5UVGELOH6IJE3MMQ734/.

Sullivan, Nate. "How Georgia Was Impacted By Civil War & Reconstruction." Study.com. https://study.com/academy/lesson/how-georgia-was-impacted-by-civil-war-reconstruction.html.

Suro, Paola. "'It Was Going to Take a Miracle:' Survivor Recounts Deadly Atlanta Hotel Fire 75 Years Later." Dec. 8, 2021. https://www.11Alive.com/article/news/local/atlanta-hotel-fire-survivor-75-years-later/85-7b7590b8-1bc7-476a-a41c-57c7971cfdcc.

Sveiven, Megan. ArchDaily. Feb. 7, 2011. https://www.archdaily.com/110019/ad-classics-high-museum-of-art-richard-meier-partners-architects.

"Swan Coach House."https://www.swancoachhouse.com/.

Team History: Atlanta Falcons. https://www.atlantafalcons.com/team/history/.

Toone, Stephanie. "10 Last-Minute Tips for the AJC Peachtree Road Race." *The Atlanta Journal-Constitution* June 26, 2019. https://www.ajc.com/lifestyles/ajc-peachtree-road-race-what-you-need-know/deldBG7bymUXFEkMH7lkZK/.

Townsend, Bob. "Beer Town: The Future of Brewing in Atlanta Isn't What It Used to Be." *The Atlanta Journal-Constitution* Sept. 4, 2019. https://www.ajc.com/entertainment/dining/the-future-brewing-atlanta-isn-what-used/Qem0QND5obqNt9VzVucA5L/.

"Truist Park—Pictures, Information and More of the Atlanta Braves Ballpark." Ballparks of Baseball. https://www.ballparksofbaseball.com/ballparks/truist-park/.

"Turner Field Stadium." MLB Teams. http://www.mlb-teams.com/stadiums/bravesStadium.php.

Tyler Perry Studios. https://tylerperrystudios.com/.

Underground Atlanta. Sept. 18, 2021. https://undergroundatl.com/.

"Upgrades to Bobby Dodd Stadium Announced." FanNation. Feb. 21, 2020. https://www.si.com/college/georgiatech/football/bobby-dodd-2020-upgrades.

"Urban Tree Canopy Study." Trees Atlanta. https://www.treesatlanta.org/resources/urban-tree-canopy-study/.

"The Varsity: Atlanta in 50 Objects: Exhibitions." Aug. 11, 2021. https://www.atlantahistorycenter.com/exhibitions/the-varsity/.

"The Varsity." https://thevarsity.com/.

Vega, Muriel. "Music Midtown: A History." *Atlanta Magazine.* Apr. 11, 2017. https://www.atlantamagazine.com/news-culture-articles/music-midtown-a-history/.

"The Vortex Bar & Grill—Best Burgers in Atlanta." Jan. 30, 2015. https://thevortexatl.com/.

"Waffle House Museum, Decatur, Georgia." RoadsideAmerica.com. https://www.roadsideamerica.com/story/18095.

Walton Gas. "What Any Georgian Should Know about Waffle House." Walton Gas. June 3, 2021. https://www.waltongas.com/what-any-georgian-should-know-about-waffle-house/.

Weiss, Joey. "The History behind Atlanta's Iconic Mary Mac's Tea Room." Atlanta Eats. Oct. 23, 2021. https://www.atlantaeats.com/blog/a-closer-look-at-atlantas-iconic-mary-macs-tea-room/.

"Welcome to Paschal's." Paschal's. https://www.paschalsatlanta.com/.

"Westin Peachtree Plaza." The Skyscraper Center. https://www.skyscrapercenter.com/building/westin-peachtree-plaza/1241.

WFMYStaff. "Waffle House Ends up with 2% of Eggs Produced." *WFMY News 2.* Aug. 15, 2005. https://www.wfmynews2.com/article/news/waffle-house-ends-up-with-2-of-eggs-produced/83-403704626.

Wheatley, Thomas. "Can Atlanta Survive Another Snowpocalypse?" *Atlanta Magazine.* Feb. 1, 2021. https://www.atlantamagazine.com/news-culture-articles/can-atlanta-survive-another-snowpocalypse/.

Wheatley, Thomas. "Georgia Breweries Come Back Strong." Axios. Sept. 19, 2022. https://www.axios.com/local/atlanta/2022/09/19/georgia-breweries-come-back-strong.

Wheatley, Thomas. "Underground Atlanta Will Try, Try Again." *Atlanta Magazine.* Mar. 17, 2021. https://www.atlantamagazine.com/news-culture-articles/underground-atlanta-will-try-try-again/.

"When Was Atlanta's Worst Snowstorm?" *Atlanta Magazine.* Nov. 23, 2019. https://www.atlantamagazine.com/list/you-asked-we-answered-34-things-you-probably-dont-know-about-atlanta/when-was-atlantas-worst-snowstorm/.

"Where Did 'Hotlanta' Come from and Why Does It Refuse to Die?" *Atlanta Magazine.* Nov. 23, 2019. https://www.atlantamagazine.com/list/you-asked-we-answered-34-things-you-probably-dont-know-about-atlanta/where-did-hotlanta-come-from-and-why-does-it-refuse-to-die/.

White, Dawn. "Atlanta Pride Festival in Full Swing after Hiatus Due to Covid-19." 11Alive.com, Oct. 9, 2022. https://www.11alive.com/article/news/local/atlanta-pride-festival-kicks-off-in-person-after-hiatus/85-bc83512c-8c2a-4379-a290-d5062e0788b8.

"Who Made America? | Innovators | Robert Woodruff." PBS. https://www.pbs.org/wgbh/theymadeamerica/whomade/woodruff_hi.html.

"Why Is Georgia Known as the Peach State?: Roundabout Atlanta." Roundabout Atlanta Tours & Transportation. Apr. 21, 2021. https://www.roundaboutatlanta.com/why-is-georgia-known-as-the-peach-state/.

"Why Is Sweet Tea Only in the South?" Southern Breeze Sweet Tea. Mar. 22, 2021. https://southernbreezesweettea.com/blogs/sweetlivin/why-is-sweet-tea-only-in-the-south.

"Why Stone Mountain Is Georgia's Most-Visited Attraction." Explore Georgia.org. Mar. 2021. https://www.exploregeorgia.org/things-to-do/article/why-stone-mountain-is-georgias-most-visited-attraction.

"Willie B.: Atlanta in 50 Objects: Exhibitions." Atlanta History Center. Nov. 19, 2020. https://www.atlantahistorycenter.com/exhibitions/atlanta-in-50-objects/willie-b/.

Willingham, A J. "What It's Really like at Dragon Con." CNN. https://www.cnn.com/interactive/2018/09/entertainment/dragon-con-cnnphotos-trnd/.

Willis, Megan. "The Guide to Colleges in Metro Atlanta: KnowAtlanta. https://www.knowatlanta.com/education/the-guide-to-colleges-in-metro-atlanta.

Wilson, Dave. "Is This Heaven? No, It's a Waffle House." ESPN. Oct. 19, 2017. https://www.espn.com/college-football/story/_/id/21067022/college-football-saturday-sec-country-waffle-house.

Wilson, Jocelyn. "A Brief History of Atlanta's Rise in Hip-Hop—Google Arts & Culture." Google Arts & Culture. https://artsandculture.google.com/story/a-brief-history-of-atlanta-39-s-rise-in-hip-hop/VgXRISv_xGKfyQ?hl=en.

"World Cup 2026: Atlanta's Mercedes-Benz Stadium Named as a Host Site." FOX 5 Atlanta. June 17, 2022. https://www.fox5atlanta.com/news/world-cup-2026-atlantas-mercedes-benz-stadium-named-as-a-host-site.

Wyatt, Kristen. "Waffle House Still Dishin' Diner Food at 50." NBC News. Aug. 15, 2005, https://www.nbcnews.com/id/wbna8927443.

Yamanouchi, Kelly. "History of an Airport: From Racetrack to World Destination." *The Atlanta Journal-Constitution* May 6, 2012. https://www.ajc.com/business/history-airport-from-racetrack-world-destination/kgHGwd54kQuSWeUZQJAHvN/.

Yeomans, Curt. "Georgia Officials Mark 10 Years since Opening of First Peach Pass Lanes in Gwinnett." *Gwinnett Daily Post.* Oct. 2, 2021. https://www.gwinnettdailypost.com/local/georgia-officials-mark-10-years-since-opening-of-first-peach-pass-lanes-in-gwinnett/article_1c0e6270-230b-11ec-9d87-3bfbef7a73f8.html.

Yeoman, Curt. "Photos: A Look Back at Interstate 285's History on the 50th Anniversary." *Gwinnett Daily Post.* Oct. 16, 2019. https://www.gwinnettdailypost.com/multimedia/photos-a-look-back-at-interstate-285s-history-on-the-50th-anniversary/collection_447259c0-efb8-11e9-b063-2f6ef37907b1.html.

Zusel, Yvonne. "Map: Breweries, Brewpubs to Try in Metro Atlanta." *The Atlanta Journal-Constitution* Mar. 4, 2022. https://www.ajc.com/blog/atlanta-restaurants/map-breweries-brewpubs-try-metro-atlanta/ow9WPOdrZ4tAcvpSxIvKXL

INDEX